The Quran

God's Word
or
Satan's Great Deception?

JOHN W. THARP

iUniverse, Inc.
Bloomington

iUniverse books may be ordered through booksellers or by contacting:

iUniverse
1663 Liberty Drive
Bloomington, IN 47403
www.iuniverse.com
1-800-Authors (1-800-288-4677)

ISBN: 978-1-4620-0749-3 (sc)
ISBN: 978-1-4620-0750-9 (hc)
ISBN: 978-1-4620-0748-6 (ebook)

Printed in the United States of America

iUniverse rev. date: 04/07/2011

To

All who love the Lord

This book is dedicated to my wife, family
and friends who gave me the encouragement
to put in writing what is on my heart.

Contents

Preface

This book is intended to be an encouragement, for the reader, to expand their knowledge of the Quran. The Quran is the doctrinal book of Cannon, for the fastest growing faith in the United States, Islam. Many people have never read it and have no knowledge of its contents.

During this research two questions quickly moved to the top of the list. First, how would the Holy Bible and the Holy Quran fair in a side by side assessment? Second, how would the Holy Quran stand up under the same disciplines of study applied to the Holy Bible?

The first question requires an examination of the major points of doctrine that separates the Holy Bible and the Holy Quran. In this comparison I will be quoting text from *"The Meaning of the Holy Quran"* by Abdullah Yusaf Ali. The text from the Holy Bible will be from *The Thompson Chain-Reference Bible*, King James Version, by Frank Charles Thompson. This book will address the comparison from the side that favors the Holy Bible. Nevertheless, it will challenge you to examine your views and beliefs in relation to the Quran.

My involvement in Biblical Studies began some forty years ago. The interest was amplified by the missionary work of my uncle Eugene in Haiti. Uncle Eugene found the local customs were directly affected by the beliefs of the people. My travels in the military brought me into contact with many different faiths around the world. Each vastly diverse from mine, which brought to life the lessons taught by my uncle. These encounters amplified my desire for a deeper study of my own faith.

I returned to school and obtained a Bachelor of Arts in Biblical Studies, graduating Magna Cum Laude. Here I applied a standard set of systematic disciplines of criticism required to examine the Holy Bible. The examination began by studying the geography, history and archeology of the bible lands. The geographical location of the Holy Bible is the same lands of the Holy Quran. Other approaches of analysis are designed to analyze the bible through a set of established criticisms. First, was the Literary Criticism which deals with the question of authorship? This is done by analyzing historical documents of the time and archeological discoveries. During the Literary Criticism process, information is gathered which is later examined under the discipline of Form Criticism. Form Criticism identifies and recognizes the different literary genres within the scriptures. The next discipline is the Redaction Criticism which studies the document in its final form.

Assessing the theological part of the authors contribution. It examines the document with regard to who edited the material that produced the work created. Finally, a Historical Criticism is applied which spans the years to get the meaning of the text that was written.

I have taken these disciplines and applied them to the Quran. What I found is put forth for your review. However, it is not an all inclusive study of the subject. There is a host of information out there to be examined. Every day archeological discoveries are revealing new information which brings more information to the research. Often when new light is shed on our own beliefs, our defense mechanism in activated. We tend to reject those finding that do not support our point of view. So it is with Islam, they will reject any fact that differs from the account within the Quran. For example, Islam claims that the Hebrew Bible was corrupted in the time of Jeremiah. Notwithstanding, the Dead Sea Scrolls, unearthed in 1947, supported the text of the Torah, which Jesus quoted. The Scrolls confirmed the text of the Hebrew Bible used at the time of Jesus. The Torah spans the time frame of 1450 B.C. through 1410 B.C. The book of Jeremiah came some 860 years later in 550 B.C.

You will find each chapter in the book is arranged in a specific order. It is designed to guide you through the historical situation that has brought us to this point in time. Beginning with how the Quran was *"Marked for Deception"* from the beginning. We must understand that there is a connection between events *"Then and Now."* How is it that those events have us *"Snared in War"*? Who is *"Muhammad"* and how was he declared the seal of the prophets? What is the process that produced *"The Quran"* that we have today? The revelations within the Quran were to have come from Gabriel. Was *"Muhammad's Gabriel"* the same Gabriel that spoke to Daniel and Mary as recorded in the Holy Bible? Looking within the Quran, for answers to these questions can be difficult, as there are many *"Contradictions within the Quran."* How does *"The Holy Bible"* stand up to the same scrutiny? Finally, what would be the compelling factor behind *"Why the Satanic Deception."*

May God the Father of our Lord Jesus the Christ bless you and guide you on your search for truth.

John Tharp

Introduction

When it came to the Quran, Muslims and Islam, what I believed was founded upon second hand information. My understanding had been molded by a media influx of information centered on the peacefulness of Islam. The main thought put forth was fixed upon a doctrinal difference between the teachings of the Quran and the actions of radical Muslims. To complicate matters what Muslims share with non-Muslims, concerning the Quran, Muslims and Islam, is not only confusing but mostly untrue. I found that comprehensive information on the three was virtually non-existent. It was then I purchased a Quran to examine the doctrine it espoused, mostly to justify the doctrinal position I held. However, as time passed and the study on the subject progressed, it became necessary to deal with the anti-Christian beliefs and practices within my own faith. To be Christian, means to be Christ like. Not just in the way we live but in our purpose, motives and objectives. Working to complete the work Jesus put us here to do, John 14:12

John 14:12 "Verily, verily, I say unto you, He that believeth on me, the works that I do shall he do also; and greater works than these shall he do; because I go unto my Father."

It was evident that the teachings of Christ had become mingled with the traditions of men. At this point let me clarify my position, my trust and belief in Jesus of Nazareth as the only *begotten Son of God and Messiah* have been more than strengthened and fully confirmed by this endeavor. What has changed is my understanding of the purpose of God, in creating humanity, the role of the scriptures, prophets, Jesus and each of us as individuals. I have come to understand "time" as God views it. I have a clear vision concerning the true outline of the Holy Bible. I have expanded my knowledge of how to see the world as God sees it, through the Scriptures. Finally, what has changed is my understanding of the full purpose and the final outcome of God's plan for humanity. The importance of Jesus, his life, death and resurrection, to that plan cannot be overstated. For all the purposes of God, are centered on Jesus as "The Christ." To my amazement all of these things are quite different from what I have been taught.

I wish to thank my wife, family and many friends who have given me encouragement. Without them I could not have finished this work. Their encouragement gave the support that kept me on course to complete this work. I pray that the blessings of God be upon them for their support.

Chapter 1

Marked for Deception

Whether one believes in Satan, is not the issue of this book. Throughout the years evil has been depicted in terms of satanic involvement. This fact is acknowledged by the Old Testament, New Testament and the Quran. As such, satanic evil leaves an unmistakable mark on everything it touches. So it is with the Quran, the mark of satanic evil is there, if you look beyond the surface, you will find it. The main instrument of evil is the lie. Within the New Testament the Greek work for *"lie"* is "Pseudos" meaning falsehood; lie, lying. It comes from the Greek word Pseudoma, meaning to utter an untruth or attempt to *deceive by falsehood, falsely*, lie. Evil then takes the lie of deception it is promoting and hides it inside doctrinal points of truth, thereby, making it harder to see and find. The Quran and Islam is this type of deception. In comparison, the Quran is like a bad tree in an orchard, one must wait for the fruit to know for sure if the tree is bad. At times, the deception is hard to find and one must wait for the fruit to determine the kind of doctrine it is. The Holy Bible tells us that you will know the tree by its fruit, for the

1

fruit marks the tree's true identity. We are now finding that the fruit of the Quran is bitter and hard to swallow, so it is with a bad tree. Satanic deception has corrupted the Islamic tree from its roots.

The unmistakable marks of satanic deception, is found within the pages of the Quran and seen in the life of Muhammad. The Quran, Islam and Muhammad all show forth the character of satanic deception. All three appeal to the worldly sensual side of this life. In one form or another, the precepts taught in the Quran, appeals to the lust of the human flesh, lusts of the human eyes and the pride of human life, all of these put together, are the totality of mankind without the truth of God in his life.

> *1 John 2:16*
> "¹⁶For all that *is* in the world, the lust of the flesh, and the lust of the eyes, and the pride of life, is not of the Father, but is of the world."

When a close examination of Muhammad's life and the Quran is made, we see that they are diametrically opposed to all that God declares pure and holy. God set forth the Ten Commandments as the standard for purity and holiness. It is no accident that the Ten Commandments have been omitted from the Quran. The Quran and Sunna declare Muhammad to be holy and pure. Notwithstanding, Muhammad's life and teachings do not hold up to that standard. In fact his life, and religion, was and is, contrary to the Ten Commandments of God. The course of study at the Faculty of Islamic Theology, University of Tehran, reveal that Muhammad was an idolater, murderer, liar, thief, child molester, and adulterer.

The evidence of his idolatry is found in the idol ritual worship that surrounds the Kaaba. The black stone and the rituals assigned came from the pre-Islamic paganism of Mecca where Muhammad was raised. They are nothing more than idol worship. Islamic documents discussed in this book, reveal how Muhammad, in an attempt to appease his family, was offering to include, *"within his new religion,"* a form of idol worship that required human sacrifice. Human sacrifice, in particular children, came from the historical culture of the Middle East. It is a practice forbidden by God in Leviticus 18:21 and Deuteronomy 12:31.

> *Leviticus 18:21*
> "²¹ And thou shalt not let any of thy seed pass through *the fire* to Molech, neither shalt thou profane the name of thy God: I *am* the LORD."

Deuteronomy 12:31

"[31] Thou shalt not do so unto the LORD thy God: for every abomination to the LORD, which he hateth, have they done unto their gods; for even their sons and their daughters they have burnt in the fire to their gods."

In addition, Muhammad tried to bargain with the Jews in Medina on how much of Judaism was going to be in *his religion.* When they rejected him and his religion, he put Ramadan in, in place of the Day of Atonement. In Islam there is no need of atonement for sins.

He became a murderer when the peoples of Arabia rejected him and his religion. Shortly after the rejection he came out of the cave and declared that God had instructed him to spread the faith with the sword. For this reason Islam was known for centuries as the religion of the sword. A fact that somehow has been deleted from present day public school history books. It was then that he [Muhammad] began attacking the caravans that moved between Mecca and Syria, killing the caravan workers and stealing the merchandise. He became a liar as his new religion which was supposed to embrace peace and life, in reality brought turmoil and death.

According to the documents and teaching of the Faculty of Islamic Theology of the University of Tehran, Muhammad's youngest wife was six when he married her; however, he waited until she was nine to consummate the marriage. This qualifies him as a child molester. By his own standards, Muhammad was an adulterer, and his tendency for not practicing what he preached, can be seen in his marriages and his teaching concerning marriage. The Quran, allowed for men to have up to four wives. After his first wife died, Muhammad married nine women and one of them a child of six. It is clear that Muhammad and Islam, as put forth in the Quran and Sunna and espoused by Islam, does not fit the description of a holy man and a holy religion of God.

Satanic deception breeds hostility. It is usually occasioned by a negative reaction to God's people. The godly life, of God's people, provokes jealousy, anger and resistance on the part of those opposed to it. It can become open hatred.

Chapter 2

Then and Now

The knowledge that Muslims share with non-Muslims concerning Muhammad and Islam, is confusing to say the least. Although they proclaim Muhammad to be an infallible man and "the perfect" prophet of God, the facts of his life do not support that declaration. The reality of actions and events that make up the sum total of Muhammad's life are contrary to Islam's proclamations. The Quran itself, records a direct contradiction between what Muhammad preached and practiced. Laying aside the life of Muhammad and concentrating on the book, *he did not write,* the Quran. Not being able to read or write Muhammad could not have known if what was written down was what he said. In contrast, the Torah of the Hebrew Bible was written by Moses. Now we begin to see why the world is in such turmoil over Muhammad's teachings, -or- were they his teachings?

Ali Bekr, his successor, delayed writing any of Muhammad's sayings for over one year after Muhammad's death. The Quran, as a book, did not appear until the third successor, Uthman released it, after much bickering over actual words of Muhammad. We also know that Ali Bekr, ordered, the prophets' sayings to be written down *as good as memory could serve.* One fact cannot be overlooked; it was not until 1924 A.D. that a Quran acceptable to the Islamic world was produced. The importance of this is Islam believes the Quran is the protected, infallible, incorruptible, and final word of God. This final Quran took over 1000 years to become acceptable to Muslims. We also know that the Sunna, a book that was to have recorded the exemplary life of the prophet, was plagued with miss quotes that served the political or religious interests of others. The relative importance of this is magnified due to the importance of these two books, (Quran and Sunna) to Islam. They represent in bodily form the major sources of practice and beliefs for Muslims.

Nevertheless, whatever Muhammad said or did the fact remains, the world has been and continues to be, under siege by the followers of Muhammad. As of this date no nation or peoples have been excluded from Islam's reign of terror. For I assert strongly that because of the teachings of the Quran, there is no such thing as a peaceful Muslim. When one reads Surah 60:1 you quickly come to understand the riots and destruction over a cartoon and the words of the Pope. All who do not embrace Islam are enemies of Allah.

Surah 60:1

"O ye who believe!
Take not My enemies
And yours as friends
(Or protectors)--offering them
(Your) love, even though
They have rejected the Truth
That has come to you.
And have (on the contrary)
Drives out the Messenger
And yourselves (from your homes),
(Simply) because ye believe
In Allah your Lord
If ye have come out
To strive in My Way
And to seek My Good Pleasure,
(Take them not as friends),
Holding secret converse
Of love (and friendship)
With them: for I know
Full well all that ye
Reveal. And any of you
That does this has strayed
From the Straight Path."

It was not radical Muslims rioting and burning over the picture in a cartoon of Muhammad or over the words of the Pope. It was the "peaceful everyday Muslims." An article released by the Associated Press, as late as June 22, 2008, reported Islamic schools in Alexandria and Fairfax, Virginia taught the children in grades K-12 that, it is permissible for Muslims to kill adulterers and converts from Islam. That Muslims are permitted to take the lives and property of those deemed polytheist. The text book used in these schools came from Saudi Arabia where the same curriculum is taught.

An identical account was reported in an article by Amy Gardner, staff writer for the Washington Post on June 24, 2008. She reported that:

> "At issue are recent reviews of teaching materials concluding that some textbooks used by the Islamic school in Fairfax contain language intolerant of Jews and other groups as well as passages that could be construed as advocating violence."

This school has a history of such teachings. On May 3, 2004, WorldNetDaily.com, posted an article titled *"Look who's Teaching Johnny about Islam"* by Paul Sperry. Mr. Sperry, an investigative reporter, found that the consultant that was,

"...shaping classroom education on Islam in American Public Schools" recently worked for a school funded and controlled by the Saudi government, which propagates a rigidly anti-western strain of Islam." Mr. Sperry identified this consultant as Susan L. Douglas. The following are items quoted from Mr. Sperry's article.

> "WorldNetDaily has learned that up until last year Douglas taught social studies at the Islamic Saudi Academy in Alexandria, VA., which teaches Wahhabism through textbooks that condemn Jews and Christians as enemies of Islam. Her husband, Usama Amer, still teaches at the grades 2-12 School, a spokeswoman there confirmed. Both are practicing Muslims"

> "Douglas, routinely described as a "scholar" or "historian," has edited manuscripts of world history textbooks used by middle and high school students across the country. She's also advised state education boards on curriculum standards dealing with world religion, and has helped train thousands of public school teachers on Islamic instruction."

"Christians and Jews repeatedly are labeled as infidels and enemies of Islam who should not be befriended or emulated, and are referred to in eight-grade textbooks as 'apes and pigs,'" the report said. In addition, it found that "some Saudi government-funded textbooks used in North American Islamic schools have been found to encourage incitement to violence against non-Muslims."

"Critics complain that Douglass, who taught at the Saudi academy for at least a decade, has convinced American textbook publishers and educators to gloss over the violent aspects of Islam to make the faith more appealing to non-Muslim children. The units on Islam reviewed by WorldNetDaily appear to give a glowing and largely uncritical view of the faith."

"The Council on Islamic Education, (CIE) is a Los Angeles-based Muslim activist group run by Shabbir Mansuri, who has been quoted in the local press saying he's waging a 'bloodless' revolution to fight what he calls anti-Muslim bias in public schools and promote Islam in a positive light in American classrooms. Mansuri, who consults with Saudi education ministers at his center, claimed in a 2002 op-ed piece that Islam has been on American soil "since before this nation was founded."

"Three major U.S. publishers of world history texts—Houghton Miffin, McGraw Hill, and Prentice Hall—have all let Mansuri and Douglass review their books. In fact, Houghton Miffin's seventh grade text, "Across the Centuries," was republished according to CIE's suggestions."

"In the past, most K-12 texts devoted no more than a few pages to Islam. But thanks to CIE's efforts since 1990–including lobbying state education boards—grades-school texts units on Islam have flourished. "Across the Centuries," for one, spends more than 30 pages on Islam and includes colorful prose and graphics."

"But it offers a sanitized version of Islam, critics say."

"For instance, the text softens the meaning of "jihad" – a concept interpreted in Abdullah

Yusuf Ali's "The Meaning of the Holy Quran" to mean "waging war," or "fighting in Allah's cause"—with dying while fighting in the cause the highest form of jihad."

"Holy war is not part of the definition found in the "Across the Centuries" textbook, however. 'An Islamic term that is often misunderstood is jihad,' the text says on page 64. The term means to 'struggle,' to do one's best to resist temptation and overcome evil."

"It's a sugar-coated definition, says Edward White, associate counsel for the Thomas More Law Center, Mich.-based public-interest law firm which has fought what it sees as Islamic indoctrination in U.S. public education."

"Even scholar John L. Esposito, considered by critics to be one of Islam's leading apologists, has written that "jihad means the struggle to spread and defend Islam"—through "warfare" if necessary.

This situation is not unique to the United States it is also present in the United Kingdom.

On July 29, 2008, The Fox News Channel show "Fox and Friends" reported that a survey was taken in England among Muslim students. The survey was taken among British Muslim students on United Kingdom campuses. What they found is, that 32% of the students say killing for Islam is justifiable, 40% support Sharia Law in United Kingdom courts and 33% support a worldwide Islamic state. This survey was taken between January 22 and February 14, 2008 and was conducted by YouGov/Center for Social Cohesion.

Within this survey we find the teachings of the Quran. Within this survey we see the example displayed in the life of Muhammad. This survey reveals the attitude behind the present day war between Muslims in general, radical Muslims, in particular, Jews and Christianity. The "Holy Jihad" is in the Quran and Muhammad is known to have started the *religion of the sword*. This religion finds its beginning preaching peace and ends in blood and war. Islam continues that tradition today, encompassing the entire world. This religion teaches that peace can only be obtained by conflict. All peoples are to submit to Islam or suffer the conflict and hostility that will be put upon you. Look at Surah 8:59-60 and the footnote that explains how you are to understand the individual Muslim responsibility to it.

Surah 8:59-60 Pages 428-429

"[59] Let not the Unbelievers
Think that they can
Get the better (of the godly),
They will never frustrate (them).
[60] Against them make ready
Your strength to the utmost
Of your power, to strike terror
Into (the hearts of) the enemies
Of Allah and your enemies
And others besides, whom
Allah doth know. Whatever
Ye shall spend in the Cause
Of Allah, shall be repaid
Unto you, and ye shall not
Be treated unjustly."[1227]

Footnote 1226 Page 429

"There are always lurking enemies whom you may not know, but whom Allah knows. *It is your duty to be ready against all, for the sacred Cause under whose banner you are fighting.*"

Surah 8:38-39 Page 423

[38] "Say to the Unbelievers,
If (now) they desist (from Unbelief),
Their past would be forgiven them;
But if they persist, the punishment
Of those before them is already
(A matter of warning for them).

[39] "And fight them on
Until there is no more
Tumult or oppression,
And there prevails
Justice and faith in Allah[1207]
Altogether and everywhere;
But if they cease, verily Allah
Doth se all that they do."[1208]

Footnote 1208 Page 423

"If they cease from fighting and from persecution of truth. Allah judges them by their
actions and their motives, and would not wish
that they should be *harassed with further hostility.* But if they refuse all terms, the righteous

have nothing to fear: Allah will help protect them."

C 38, Page 11:

"And so his very virtues and loyalties pointed
To offence and conflict, mockery and misrepresentation.
Hatred and persecution, threats, tortures, and exile
For him and his, and martyrdoms, wars, revolutions.
And the shaking of the foundations of history
And the social order. *But Islam meant the willing submission of his will to Allah, The active attainment of peace through conflict.*"

Surah 8:17 Page 412

"It is not ye who
Slew them; it was Allah:…"

Surah 8:65 Page 430

"O Prophet! arouse the Believers
To the fight. If there are
Twenty amongst you, patient
And persevering, they will
Vanquish two hundred: if a hundred,

They will vanquish a thousand
Of the Unbelievers: for these
Are a people without understanding."

I pray that all who read this book will gain a new insight into the conflict that has been thrust upon all humanity.

It is difficult to discuss the conflict between Islam, Christians and Jews without crossing the boundaries of doctrine which separates them. All are connected in two major areas, first, each religion believes in one God, and that God is Jehovah to the Jews and Christians and Allah to Islam. Nevertheless, it is supposed to be the same God. Second, each uses the Hebrew Bible (Old Testament) as one of their major sources of inspiration and guidance. Christians add to it the New Testament. Muslims add the Quran to both the Old and New Testament making what Islam calls the "Whole Book of Allah". The conflict arises over the interpretation of the circumstances surrounding the everlasting covenant made by God with Abraham, of a "seed" to Abraham which could not be numbered and who would possess the Promised Land, now occupied by Jordan, Syria, Lebanon, Saudi Arabia, and in part by Egypt and Iraq.

The word "seed" here is very important because both Muslims and Jews would rather use the word "descendant."

Jews view this descendent as through Isaac. Islam views this descendant as through Ishmael. Christians view Jesus as the final descendant through Isaac. Christians believe that Jesus, through grace, has grafted in all whom except him as the Messiah, as part of the seed. Therefore Christians are heirs and joint heirs with Christ Jesus.

> *Romans 8:16-17* " 16 The Spirit itself beareth witness with our spirit, that we are the children of God:17 And if children, then heirs; heirs of God, and joint heirs with Christ; if so be that we suffer with him, that we may be also glorified together."

Jews (decedents of Isaac) and Arabs (decedents of Ishmael) are locked in a physical battle over this worlds promise land. According to Genesis 13; Abraham and Lot were at a spot between Bethel and Hai when God separated them. At this spot Abraham was instructed to look North, South, East and West and as far as he could see was to be his and his "seed" forever. Genesis 15:18 gives a physical description of this promise land, from the "River of Egypt" in the South, to the "Euphrates River" in the North.

> *Genesis 15:18* "In the same day the Lord made a covenant with Abram, saying, Unto thy seed

have I given this land, from the river of Egypt unto the great river, the river Euphrates:"

This land runs from the southernmost part of Saudi Arabia to the Euphrates river in Iraq. This land became the inheritance of the "first born son" of Abraham through Sarah and not Hagar.

> *Genesis 17:19* "And God said, *Sarah* thy wife shall bear thee a son indeed; and thou shalt call his name Isaac: and I will establish my covenant with him for an everlasting covenant, and with his seed after him."

> *Genesis 21:9-10* "9 And Sarah saw the son of Hagar the Egyptian, which she had born unto Abraham, mocking.10 Wherefore she said unto Abraham, Cast out this bondwoman and her son: for the son of this bondwoman shall not be heir with my son, even with Isaac."

Here in Genesis we find the beginning of the conflict between these two sons of Abraham. Ishmael is mocking Isaac over the birthright of the first born, an argument that continues to the present day. It is here that the roots of satanic deception were sown. Arabs embrace Muhammad, as the descendant of Ishmael, and his teachings as the avenue by which they can unify and gain possession of this land and the world. This is the root cause for the hatred of Israel. Ishmael, (Arabs) want Isaac and his descendants dead and thereby remove them once and for all from claiming ownership of this land. It is there that Satan, has found a willing accomplice in the Arabic people who already possess a fierce love of fighting, a fanaticism that has proved irresistible for them.

The conflict rages on because modern day Muslims have chosen to ignore the fact that even the Quran promises this land to the Jews.

Surah 7:137, Pages 381 & 382

"And We made a people,
Considered weak (and of no account)
Inheritors of lands
In both East and West—
Lands whereon We sent
Down Our blessings.
The fair promise of thy Lord
Was fulfilled for the Children
Of Israel, because they had
Patience and constancy,
And We leveled to the ground

21

The Great Works and fine Buildings
Which Pharaoh and His people
Erected (with such pride.)"

Surah 17:104, Page 703

"And We said thereafter
To The Children of Israel,
"Dwell securely in the land
(Of Promise)":..."

Israel is the name conferred upon Jacob, son of Isaac, after he wrestled with the angel of the Lord. It is also the biblical name given to all born to the twelve sons of Israel, the "Children of Israel." How then can we call this religion "a religion of peace?" Islam denies that which is in its own cannon of beliefs. Once again Islam is using terror and death to force it's will upon those who do not embrace it or its beliefs. Here again we find that there is no change in the religion that started with a sword and continues that practice today.

Because most people do not have a Quran close at hand, the text quoted from the Quran is listed in the bibliography. All references to the Holy Bible will be from the King James Version also listed in the bibliography. The chapters are few, because it is almost impossible to separate the subject matter into different topics. Each topic contains some elements from others. Therefore, repetitions and the occasional mingling of topics occurs, your forgiveness is requested.

Chapter Three

Snared in War

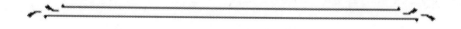

The writing of this book began with a single purpose in mind. That was, to expose Islam as an, Anti-Christian religion and, the Quran as a Book inspired by satanic influences. However, as time passed and the study on the subject progressed, it was found that I had to deal with the Anti-Christian beliefs and practices within my own faith. The Holy Bible sets the standard believers, to be a Christian means to be Christ like. Not just in the way we live but in our purpose, motives and objectives, working to complete the work Jesus put us here to do, John 14:12:

> *John 14:12* "Verily, verily, I say unto you, He that believeth on me, the works that I do shall he do also; and greater works than these shall he do; because I go unto my Father."

It has become evident that the teachings of Christ have become mingled with the traditions of men. At this point let me make this clear, my trust and belief in Jesus of Nazareth as the only *begotten* Son of God and Messiah have been more than strengthened and fully confirmed by this endeavor. What has changed is my understanding of the purpose of God, in creating humanity. I now realize the importance of each individual to the purpose of God. I have come to understand how the scriptures [Law, Prophets, Writings and New Testament], fit into that plan. I have come to understand "time" as God views it. I have come to understand the true outline of the Holy Bible and how to see the world as God sees it, through the Scriptures. Finally, what has changed is my understanding of the full purpose and the final outcome of God's plan for humanity. Also, the importance of Jesus, his life, his death and his resurrection, to that plan cannot be overstated. Every part of the purpose of God is fixed on Jesus, as "The Christ." To my amazement that purpose is quite different from what I have been taught. Muhammad did not comprehend the true meaning of Jesus as the Christ, and thereby opened himself up to the satanic deception, which is now, behind the current world unrest.

As I contemplated current events, which has the world locked in what seems to be a never-ending battle between peoples, all in the name of God. With Jews, Muslims and Christians calling each other evil and claiming to be the sole legitimate people of God. With each holding on to the promise God made to Abraham, as their claim to being the legitimate heirs to that promise.

With all of these religions laying claim to God and the Abraham covenant as the authority behind their code of ethics and practice, how is it that we find ourselves on opposite sides in a war? There is only one way to research this subject, one must look into the writings which hold the basis for their beliefs.

The TaNaKa for Jews, The Holy Bible for Christians and the Quran for Muslims. There is one book that Jews, Christian and Muslims hold in common. The TaNaK, is the Hebrew Bible also known as the Old Testament. The Hebrew Bible is often referred to by the acronym TaNaK (Torah, Neibiim and Kethubim), the Hebrew words for the three in the grouping, the Law, Prophets and Writings. Muhammad claims that his authority is rooted in the prophecies found in the Old Testament and to some in the New Testament. However, Islamic perspective of the Old and New Testaments is quite different from that of Jews and Christians.

Christianity holds its claim of authority on the deity of Jesus as "The Christ", "the Messiah." Proclaiming Jesus as "The Christ," "the Messiah," "Lord" and "only begotten Son of God" are facts that Muhammad and Islam denounce with great force. Orthodox Jews also reject Jesus as the Messiah. Sometimes it appears that even Christians have forgotten, that "Christ" is not the surname of Jesus but it is his title. He is Jesus "The Christ" and the "Son of God." This point is very important as Muhammad claims to be the last and final prophet. Muhammad claims that he supersedes all prophets, including Jesus. Muhammad claims that Jesus was just a prophet and not the Christ and certainly not the son of God. In fact he does not believe that a messiah is needed at all. Muhammad even goes so far as to say that Jesus commanded everyone to follow him (Muhammad). Surah 61:6 and footnotes 5437, page 1461

Surah 61:6 Page 1461

"And remember, Jesus,
The son of Mary, said:
"O Children of Israel!
I am the messenger of Allah
(Sent) to you, [5436] confirming [5437]
The Law (which came)
Before me, and giving
Glad Tidings of a Messenger
To come after me,
Whose name shall be Ahmad," [5438]
But when he came to them
With Clear Signs, [5439]
They said, "This is

Evident sorcery!"

Footnote 5438; Page 1461

"Amhad", or "Muhammad", the Praised One, is almost a translation of the Greek word Periclytos. In the present Gospel of John, 14:16, 15:26 and 16:7, the word "Comforter" in the English version is for the Greek word "Paracletos", which means "Advocate", "one called to the help of another, a kind friend", rather than "Comforter". Our doctors contend that Paracletos is a corrupt reading for Periclytos, and that in their original saying of Jesus there was a prophecy of our Holy Prophet *Ahmad* by name. Even if we read Paracelete, it would apply to the Holy Prophet, who is "a Mercy for all creatures" (21:107) and "most kind and merciful to the Believers" (9:128).

Herein is the basis for Christians labeling Islam as anti-Christian or antichrist, for if Muhammad accepted Jesus as "The Christ" then there would be no need for a last and final Prophet? For Muhammad, it is here that the satanic influence began.

There is a million ways to tell a lie but only one way to tell the truth. Evil has many faces to hide behind while good has only one and it must be out front. In addition, evil has one major attribute; it always accuses the good of attacking and committing wickedness against it. When the fact is, it's the other way around. It is the evil who is working the wickedness against the good. In other words, evil will tell a lie, and then accuse the good of lying. This applies to all atrocities that evil in any form, commits against man and God.

It is abundantly clear that the present conflict is between the two major religions of the world, Christianity and Islam. It can be said that the world is in a tug of war between the followers of Jesus "The Christ" and Muhammad. Nevertheless, both hold their legitimacy on a set of spiritual values found in the Old Testament. Christianity holds its legitimacy in the lineage of Isaac while the Islam [Muhammadans] on the lineage of Ishmael. Isaac being the son of Abraham through Sarah, his wife, and Ishmael is Abraham's son through Sarah's hand maid, Hegar, an Egyptian. All this leaves the world in a dilemma, because, these two religions encompass the majority of the world's population and as such, affect every nation on earth.

Here in the United States the dilemma is even more acute as we claim to have a government which has successfully separated the church from the state. A point which I maintain is factually and practically, impossible. For Islam there is only one law for individuals and state, the Quran.

The dilemma arises when we send representatives to our governmental bodies, be it Local, State or Federal. Those people will make and pass laws based on their value system. Simply put, we can send Godly people who will pass good laws or send the ungodly who will make and pass bad laws. This statement can be made because both the major religions, Christianity and Islam, assert that God is the basis of all laws that are good. With both claiming the other to be evil, we then seem doomed to this eternal battle between them. Nevertheless, the Quran requires Muslims to include its teachings in the laws of the land. The Holy Bible does not. Therefore, if we elect Muslims into public office they must include the Islamic doctrine in the laws they make. The differences between Christianity and Islam are clear as day and night. Nevertheless, both claim to be the true representatives of God. How then, do we determine which one is in fact the true representative of God and which is not? Here we begin our research into the Quran, Muhammad, and Islam.

Chapter Four

Muhammad

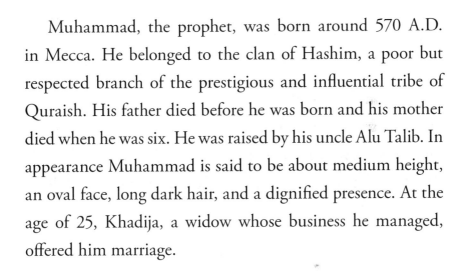

Muhammad, the prophet, was born around 570 A.D. in Mecca. He belonged to the clan of Hashim, a poor but respected branch of the prestigious and influential tribe of Quraish. His father died before he was born and his mother died when he was six. He was raised by his uncle Alu Talib. In appearance Muhammad is said to be about medium height, an oval face, long dark hair, and a dignified presence. At the age of 25, Khadija, a widow whose business he managed, offered him marriage.

Muhammad is said to have been, withdrawn and pensive in temperament. He like his fellow tribesmen became a trader and made several journeys working on caravans going from Mecca to Syria. It was here that he met and conversed with Christians and Jews. This encounter was amplified by the Roman occupation of Israel. Many Christian and Jews fled into Arabia to escape the Roman rule. In addition, the peoples of Arabia were well aware of the Greek Culture brought to Arabia by Alexander the Great. What Muhammad knew about the Jewish and Christian beliefs came from his contact with them. His personal religious beliefs came from the Pre-Islamic paganism of Mecca. His tribe, the Quraish, was the keepers of the Kaaba Temple and the Black Stone located in Mecca.

How is it then, that Muhammad, an Arab, lays claim to being the last in a long list of Jewish prophets in the Old and New Testaments? The Quran lists twenty-eight prophets, twenty-two from the Old Testament, three from the New Testament, which included Jesus, and three from outside the Bible, one of which was Alexander the Great, *Surah 18:83-98*. Muhammad taught that the prophets started with Adam, and proceeded through Moses to Jesus and then ended with him.

At times, Mohammed would become troubled by the messages he heard at religious fairs in Mecca. Plagued by questions he would periodically withdraw to a cave outside Mecca. It was during one of these retreats that he claims to have been visited by the Archangel Gabriel, who proclaimed him a prophet of God. Mohammed's message is based on the principle that the Quran is to be the last revealed book and him to be the last of the prophets, consummating and superseding all earlier ones. In another chapter we will examine Muhammad's Gabriel.

The year 622 was one of the lowest times in Mohammed's life and fortunes, although it marks the start of his success as a religious leader. This was the year of the Hegira (flight) and all Muslims reckon this year as year one. Mohammed's flight came just as his enemies, and even his own family, were planning to assassinate him. The attempts on his life forced Muhammad and his followers to flee from Mecca to Medina. This period in time supports the end of Mohammed's persecution in Mecca and the creation of a conquering religious organization in Medina. However, during the first year in Medina, the emigrant Muslims were desperately poor, for they fled Mecca empty handed. They depended upon the charity of Medina for food and shelter. They were down to eating dates and water because they had nothing there to cook. The situation improved when Muhammad had a revelation in which Allah, speaking through Gabriel, ordered Muslims to attack the unbelievers. Any Muslim, who died in such a battle Muhammad declared, would go straight to paradise without having to wait for the judgment day. These are two of the most important Surahs in the Quran. The first turned Islam into an aggressive, warlike religion, and the second inspired the Muslims to fight with reckless fury.

After holding off an attack on Medina in 627 A.D., by Mecca, Mohammed's army gained confidence. In 630 A.D., his forces marched on Mecca and from this time on Islam spread throughout the region. He conquered Mecca then he expelled two of the Jewish tribes that opposed him and had all the males of the remaining tribe massacred.

There are several reasons for the rapid spread of Islam. First of all, Muhammad taught that any Muslim dying in battle for the faith was assured entrance into paradise, bypassing the judgment day. This sanctification of warfare appealed to Arabs and gave legitimacy to their love of fighting. The Muslim love of war was fueled by Mohammed's description of the life in the "the Garden of Delight:" Notice that the reward appeals to the flesh of mankind in this world.

Surah 56:15-26

"Upon inwrought couches,
Reclining thereon, face to face.
Youths ever-young shall go unto them round
About
With goblets and ewers and a cup of flowing
Wine,
Their [heads] shall ache not with it, neither
Shall they be drunken;
And fruits of the [sorts] which they shall
Choose,
And the flesh of birds of the [kinds] which

They shall desire.

And damsels with eyes like pearls laid up

We will give them as a reward for that which

They have done.

Therein shall they hear no vain discourse nor

Accusation of sin,

But [only] the saying, "Peace! Peace!"

> *NOTE:* The above quote was taken from "Civilization Past and Present" which included this excerpt from a Quran translated by Marmaduke Pickthall, 1937. Later we will look at the same quote from a later translation by 'Abdullah Yusuf 'Ali, because they are translated differently. Marmaduke William Muhammad Pickthall, "Meaning of the Glorious Quran", London 1356/1937

Muhammad began his ministry at the age of 40 and passed away twenty-two years later in 632 A.D. at the age of 62. After Mohammed's death, his followers began to embellish the story of his life with mythology. The story of Mohammed's ascension to heaven from Jerusalem was modeled after the ascension of Jesus. When in fact Muhammad became ill in June of 632 A.D. and died. He was buried beneath the floor of his hut in Medina. This is the second most holy shrine in

Islam. In another story, Mohammed's heart was miraculously cleansed of all unworthy thought when he was a boy of 12 and he was declared immune from error.

Muhammad was stirred by contemplations of those themes that attract the religious mind. For a considerable time after he received his commission, Muhammad endeavored to gain converts merely by persuasion. However, he had no credibility as a spiritual leader with almost everyone he met. After three years of preaching his disciples numbered only forty.

Muhammad and his message were rejected by his family in Mecca. So intense was the rejection that he fled to Medina to save his life. His cause was warmly embraced by the people of Medina. Here he evolved into a lawgiver, moral teacher and warrior. He declared it to be the will of Allah that the new faith should be spread by the sword.

Within ten years from the time of the assumption of the sword Mecca had been conquered, and the new creed established widely among the independent tribes of Arabia.

For one century after the death of Muhammad the caliphs, or successors of the prophet, embarked on an almost unbroken series of conquests. Persia, Syria, Egypt and North Africa all fell under the sword of the prophet. By 711 A.D. Spain came under attack and the provinces of Seville, Cordova, Toledo, and Granada became predominately Arabic in dress, manners, language, and religion.

Muhammad as a minister of peace and love lasted just three years while the ministry of the sword is still advancing.

Chapter Five

The Quran

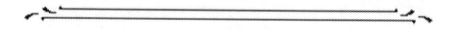

Christians view Islam as antichrist, because of Mohammed's (Islam's) rejection of Jesus as the "Son of God," "the Christ," and claim that his (Mohammed's) teachings supersedes that of Jesus. However, this is not the only reason for Christianities dim view of Islam. A complete research into Muhammad and the Quran reveals a religion that is a curious mixture of Greek Mythology, Judaism, Christianity and the pre-Islamic Paganism, of Mecca, from which Muhammad came. For Mohammed's emergent religion was rooted in the pre-Islamic traditions such as the pilgrimage and the Kaaba Shrine which were absorbed in a modified form. In reforming the pre-Islamic traditions, Muhammad also confirmed it and included this form of idolatry into Islam.

Here we will begin our research into the Quran and Islam. We must first understand how Muhammad and those who followed him viewed the "Hebrew Bible," and its authenticity, and its connection to the Quran. The following quotes are from the Quran and its commentary found in the following: "The Meaning of the Holy Quran," listed in the bibliography.

How is it concluded that the Quran is the product of satanic influence upon Muhammad? To answer this we must examine the life of Muhammad and the book, he could not write, along with the angel Gabriel. Gabriel is purported to be the angel that spoke the revelations of the Quran to Muhammad. First of all Muhammad was unlearned and could not read or write *(Surah 7:158 and footnote 1132, page 390-391).*

158 "Say: "O men! I am sent [1131]
Unto you all, as the Messenger
Of Allah, to Whom belongeth
The dominion of the heavens
And the earth: there is no god
But He: it is He that giveth
Both life and death. So believe
In Allah and His Messenger,
The unlettered Prophet, [1132]
Who believeth in Allah
And His Words: follow him
That (so) ye may be guided."

Footnote 1132:

"'Unlettered,' as applied to the Prophet here and in verse 157 above, has three special significations. (1) He was not versed in human learning; yet he was full of the highest wisdom, and had a most wonderful knowledge of the previous Scriptures. This was proof of his inspiration."

As you can see, Muhammad did not personally write any part of the Quran. About one year after his death, his close friend Aba Bekr, also the first successor of Muhammad, ordered the prophets teachings to be compiled as accurately as memory permitted. Immediately, disputes arose over the actual words of the prophet and continued until the third successor to Muhammad, Uthman, issued an official text. Uthman sent every Muslim province one copy of what he had produced. He [Uthman], at the same time, ordered all other Quranic materials burned. The Uthman text was never actually codified. Even if Muhammad were alive at this time he could not have proof read the written Quran for accuracy.

There was no written text of the Quran while Muhammad was still alive. The revelations came in bits and pieces over a 13 year period starting in Mecca and ending in Medina. The book itself has risen to the status of an idol. Rituals for approaching and handling the "sacred book" have emerged. Before it can be touched rituals for purification including washing and preparing the mind, body and spirit must be performed. The Quran cannot come into contact with any unclean substance, and at all cost must never be laid upon the ground. Nevertheless, the origins of the book and its compilations and the official text we have today, did not exist until 1924. So the Quran has been in the writing stage from Mohammed's death in 632 A.D. until 1924, some 1292 years later. It's hard to believe that an official text, of the Quran for the Islamic world, did not exist until the 20th century when an Egyptian edition was printed.

Arabic can be written without vowels. For centuries the Quran was transcribed without symbols to represent the missing vowels which allowed for more than one reading of the text. Some words could be read in different ways, because, the earliest copies of the Quran were translated without symbols to represent certain vowels. Despite the consensus among Muslim scholars on the authority of the Uthmanic text, seven or more legitimate readings of the Quran prevailed during this time. All this brings into question the validity of the Quran itself and what Muslims call "the sciences of the Quran." Which is a very strict requirement, a person must adhere to, to become a commentator and discuss the theological and legal issues of the Quran. A person must be well versed in several disciplines and sub-disciplines of this science known as the Tafsir. This science even extends to the study of grammar, lexicography, and history.

How could this be possible, as there was no unified, official or universal text in existence for 1292 years? How is it possible with seven or more renderings of the Quran being accepted over this time? How is it possible that this so called infallible word of God could not be put together for more than a millennium? How do we know that the reading we have today is the original that Muhammad recited? Muhammad was not there to settle the disputes. All this flies in the face of *Surah 19:97, page 763.*

97 "So have We made
The (Quran) easy
In thine own tongue,
That with it thou mayest give
Glad tidings to the righteous,
And warnings to the people
Given to contention."

NOTE: Why is it that the Quran uses the Old English vernaculars i.e., thine and mayest, and thou, that did not exist in Mohammed's day.

According to Islamic tradition it was the angel Gabriel who was to have spoken the words of God to the prophet Muhammad. Which, Muhammad was able to recite exactly as it had been given to him. A fact that proves false after a close examinations. This reveals a dark side of the prophet's revelations.

For quite some time after receiving his commission to preach, Muhammad endeavored to spread the word by mere persuasion. However, he had no credibility as a man of faith and by the end of three years his disciples numbered only forty.

The peoples of the times were not inclined to accept a teaching that required the renouncing of their current practices, be it Christian, Jew or pagan. Keep in mind that the population where he lived was made up of Christians and Jews that had fled the Roman occupation and the local peoples, who followed a pagan belief in polytheism.

The reaction of Mecca was to persecute Muhammad to the point he fled to Yathrib (later Medina) to avoid assassination. The new teaching proved very unpopular to most Meccans, who saw a distinct threat to the city's lucrative pilgrimage trade centered about the many-idled Kaaba. This was the responsibility of Mohammed's tribe of Quraish. About this time Mohammed's popularity was at its lowest and to complicate matters for him, Khadijh his wife died. Down and out in Mecca he fled to Medina in 622 A.D., which became known at the Hegira.

Medina was a city troubled by tribal feuds and they asked Muhammad to arbitrate the feuds, offering him considerable authority. A task he completed with a good deal of success. It was then that Muhammad began to incorporate the teaching of Judaism, Christianity into the Pre-Islamic Paganism to establish himself as a legitimate prophet of God. Soon after he declared it to be the will of God *his new faith should be spread by the sword.* Now with his cause warmly espoused by the inhabitants of Medina, Muhammad assumed along with the character of law giver and moral teacher—that of a warrior. The year following the hegira he began to attack and plunder the caravans passing from Mecca to Syria. In 630 A.D. Mohammed's forces marched on Mecca. Muhammad has now violated almost every part of the Ten Commandments, becoming a thief and murderer.

Muhammad now finds himself in a situation where he has mixed the four religious beliefs and cultures which had dominated the area for centuries, and has taken up the sword to convince people to change beliefs. He now adds one more element to this message, convert to Islam or die. These actions do not fit picture of a gentle, withdrawn, pensive boy, with a pure heart.

There was one final point Muhammad needed to establish him as the new spiritual leader. He proclaimed himself to be the final word in all religions. Therefore, Muhammad proclaimed the Quran as the last and final word from God and himself as the last and final prophet of God. His Quran divided the world into three parts; the house of Islam, where Muslims are ascendant; the house of peace those powers with whom Muslims have peace agreements; and the house of war, the rest of the world.

To accomplish this, it became necessary to associate himself with the teachings of both Jews and Christians. In Surah 3:3 Page 126 and C55 Page 131, Muhammad acknowledges the Law of Moses and the Gospel of Jesus.

Surah 3:3

"It is He Who sent down
To thee (step by step),
In truth, the Book,
Confirming what went before it;
And He sent down the Law
(Of Moses) and the Gospel 344 (Of Jesus)"

C 55:

"If the people who received
Earlier revelations confine themselves
To partial truths, and in their pride
Shut their eyes to the whole of the Book
Of Allah, their day is done;
Let the Muslims seek the society
And friendship of their own, and trust
In Allah, who knows all, and holds
Every soul responsible for its own deeds."

This was accomplished by preaching that Muslims and Islam were part of the "Peoples of the Books" referring to the Hebrew Bible (Old Testament) and the Christian addition to it, the New Testament. One area of Satanic influence on Muhammad and the Quran can be found when a close examination of the method by which these books are accepted. In order for Mohammed's new religion to be accepted the people must see a need to abandon their present belief. In the case of the Jews, Muhammad attacked the credibility of the Jews as it relates to the Hebrew Bible. He accused the Jews of corrupting the word of God. Muhammad preached that because the Jews corrupted the word God sent them. God had sent him, [Muhammad] to put the people back on the straight path to God. In the case of the Christians, Muhammad must strip Jesus of his deity and title as the son of God and messiah. In order to do this he needed to establish a new purpose of the ministry of Jesus, and that would be proclaiming Muhammad as his successor and the final authority. Mohammed's new religious book was to be a simple book combining the Old Testament, New Testament and his teachings to make the "Whole Book of Allah,"—The Quran. The following quotes from the Quran and New Testament are submitted in support of these statements. Early in the Quran, Muhammad attacks the reliability and credibility of both Jews and Jesus:

Muhammad's Disagreement with the Old Testament and Jews:

Surah 2:87-90, C. 47 Pages 40-42:

Surah 2:87-90:

" [87] We gave Moses the Book
And followed him up
With a succession of Messengers:
We gave Jesus, the son of Mary, [90]
Clear (Signs) and strengthened him
With the Holy Spirit. Is it
That whenever there comes to you
A Messenger with what ye

Yourselves desire not, ye are
Puffed up with pride?—
Some ye called imposters,
And others ye slay! [91]

[88] They say, "Our hearts
Are the wrappings [92] (which preserve
Allah's Word: we need no more)."
Nay, Allah's curse in on them
For their blasphemy:[99]
Little is it they believe.

[89] And when there comes to them
A Book [94] from Allah, confirming
What is with them—although
From of old they had prayed
For victory against those
Without Faith—when there comes
To them that which they
(Should) have recognized.
They refused to believe in it
But the curse of Allah
Is on those without Faith.

[90] Miserable is the price
For which they have sold

Their souls, in that they
Deny (the revelation) Which
Allah has sent down,
In insolent envy that Allah
Of His Grace should send it
To any of His servants He pleases:

95 Thus have they drawn
On themselves Wrath upon Wrath,
And humiliating is the punishment
Of those who reject Faith."

C. 47 page 40:

"The people of Moses and the people of Jesus
were given revelations, but alas! They played
false with their own lights And, in their self-
ishness, made narrow Allah's universal message.
To them It seemed incredible that His light
Should illumine Arabia and reform the world.
But His ways are wondrous, And they are clear
to those who have Faith."

This Surah shows the seed of deception sown in the midst
of truth. It is quite true that the Jews had "played false" with
God and violated the very heart of the Mosaic Law. As for

the Christians there were several disputes between Christian Jews and Gentile Christians, such as the issue of circumcision. However, the deception creeps in when Muhammad proclaims himself and Arabia the light of the world contrary to the teachings of Christ. John 1: 4-5 (Referring to Jesus)

> John 1:4-5 "4 In him was life; and the life was the light of men. [5] And the light shineth in darkness; and the darkness comprehended it not."

Muhammad tries to take the light of Christ and shine it upon himself. In the following Muhammad attempts to steal the light of Jesus and the birthright of Christ, just as Ishmael tried to steal the birth right of Isaac.

Quoting C. 68, pages 233 & 234;

"The People of the Book went wrong;
The Jews in breaking their Covenant,
And slandering Mary and Jesus,
And in their usury and injustice;
And the Christians in raising
Jesus the Messenger to equality
With Allah. Allah's revelation
Is continued in the Quran,
Which comes with manifest proof

And a clear light to those who understand."

Surah 4:171, pages 239-240:

"O People of the Book!
Commit no excesses [675]
In your religion: nor say
Of Allah aught but the truth.
Christ Jesus the son of Mary
Was (no more than)
A Messenger of Allah,
And His Word,
Which He bestowed on Mary,
And a Spirit proceeding
From Him: so believe
In Allah and His Messengers.
Say not "Trinity": desist. [676]
It will be better for you:
For Allah is One God:
Glory be to Him:
(Far Exalted is He) above
Having a son. To Him
Belong all things in the heavens
And on earth. And enough
Is Allah as a Disposer of affairs."

Footnote 676, page 239:

"Christ's attributes are mentioned: (1) that he was the son of a woman. Mary, and therefore a man; (2) but a messenger, a man with a mission from Allah, and therefore entitled to honour; (3) a Word bestowed on Mary, for he was created by Allah's word "Be (kun), and he was; 3:59; (4) a spirit proceeding from Allah, but not Allah: his life and his mission were more limited than in the case of some other Messerners, though we must pay equal honour to him as a Prophet of Allah. The doctrines of Trinity, equality with Allah, and sonship, are repudiated as blasphemies. Allah is independent of all needs and has no need of a son to manage His affairs. The Gospel of John (whoever wrote it) has put in a great deal of Alexandrian and Gnostic mysticism round the doctrine of the Word (Greek, Logos), but it is simply explained here."

The meaning of the following quote is clear. It is intended to render the Hebrew Bible quiescent. Islam does not attempt to annul it because parts of it are required to support their claim of legitimacy.

Appendix II, page 289

> "In the reign of Josiah about 622 B.C., certain priests and scribes (with Jeremiah the prophet) promulgated a new code, pretending that they had found it in the Temple (2 Kings 22:8). This law (*Torah*=Tawrah) was the basis of Judaism the new religion then found in Palestine."

Present day Islamic thinking is set in concrete, so much so, that any archeological finds and/or scientific research are sifted through and for the most part rendered mute. The end result excludes any information that will not support the Quran's version of facts. The following is a quote, also from Appendix II page 289, and was made referring to the archeological finds and scientific data concerning signature text.

> "We are entitled to accept the general results of a scientific examination of documents, probabilities, and dates, even though *we reject the premise which we believe to be false,* viz., that Allah does not send inspired Books through inspired Prophets. We believe that Moses existed; that he was an inspired man of God; that he gave a message which was afterwards distorted or lost; that attempts were made by Israel at various times to reconstruct that message; and that the

Towrah as we have it is (in view of the statements in 2 Esdra) no earlier than the middle of the fifth century B.C."

The two quotes above are quite revealing as Islam proclaims God to be all powerful and no power exists separate from him, Surah 3:26.

Surah 3:26, page 133:

"Say: 'O Allah!
Lord of Power (and Rule),
Thou givest Power
To whom Thou Pleasest,
And Thou strippest off Power
From whom Thou Pleasest:
Thou enduest with honour
Whom Thou Pleasest,
And Thou bringest low
Whom Thou pleasest:
In Thy hand is all Good.[369]
Verily, over all things
Thou hast power".

Nevertheless, here the Islamic teachings advance the notion of a limitation of Gods power. Because, he (Allah) could not protect his inspired book, (Old Testament). From being destroyed and/or corrupted by "mere" man, i.e., the Jews, whom he (Allah) had created. In this case we are asked to believe that the created was more powerful than his creator. This is a contradiction to Surah 15:9 and footnote 1944, page 621:

Surah 15:9 page 621:

"We have, without doubt,
Sent down the Message;
And We will assuredly
Guard it (from corruption)."

Footnote 1944 page 621:

"The purity of the text of the Quran through fourteen centuries is a foretaste of the eternal care with which Allah's Truth is guarded through all ages. All corruption's, inventions, and accretions pass away, but Allah's Pure and Holy Truth will never suffer eclipse even though the whole world mocked at it and was bent on destroying it."

More Questions to be answered: First, if Allah could not guard the Hebrew Bible from corruption how is he going to guard the Quran from the same fate? Second, remember it took 1292 years to get the final Quran, which version is guarded? The creditability of the Surah's falls into question as Arabs in Muhammad's day did not use the words, thine, thou, mayest, or bringest. These words are found in the 1611 version of the King James Holy Bible.

Muhammad's Rejection of Jesus as the Son of God:

Surah 61:6, footnote 5438; page 1461:

"And remember, Jesus,
The son of Mary, said:
"O Children of Israel!
I am the messenger of Allah
(Sent) to you, [5436] confirming [5437]
The Law (which came)
Before me, and giving
Glad Tidings of a Messenger
To come after me,
Whose name shall be Ahmad ." [5438]
But when he came to them
With Clear Signs, [5439]
They said, "This is
Evident sorcery!"

Footnote 5438;

" 'Amhad', or 'Muhammad', the Praised One, is almost a translation of the Greek word Periclytos. In the present Gospel of John 14:16, 15:26 and 16:7, the word "Comforter" in the English version is for the Greek word 'Paracletos', which means 'Advocate', 'one called to the help of another, a kind friend', rather than 'Comforter', Our doctors contend that Paracletos is a corrupt reading for Periclytos, and that in their original saying of Jesus there was a prophecy of our Holy Prophet Ahmad by name. Even if we read Paracelete, it would apply to the Holy Prophet, who is "a Mercy for all creatures" (21:107) and "most kind and merciful to the Believers" (9:128)."

First, Surah 61:6 clearly states that Jesus came to "confirm the Law" or the Old Testament which Islam denies. Now then, does the New Testament scriptures identified in the footnote above really refer to Muhammad or Jesus? Let's look and see:

John 14:16 "And I will pray the Father, and he shall give you another Comforter, that he may abide with you for ever;"

John 15:26 "But when the Comforter is come, whom I will send unto you from the Father, even the Spirit of truth, which proceedeth from the Father, he shall testify of me:"

John 16:7 "Nevertheless I tell you the truth; It is expedient for you that I go away: for if I go not away, the Comforter will not come unto you; but if I depart, I will send him unto you."

John14:26 "But the Comforter, which is the Holy Ghost, whom the Father will send in my name, he shall teach you all things, and bring all things to your remembrance, whatsoever I have said unto you."

The Greek definition of Comforter: Strong's Concordance, Greek [3875]: Parakletos (par-ak'-lay-tos); an intercessor, consoler: -- advocate, Comforter'

The New Testament scriptures mentioned above, which Muhammad uses to declare himself as the "Comforter" clearly eliminate him as the object of the position. Muhammad was applying these to himself in this earthly body of flesh. John 14:16 clearly states that the comforter would abide with you forever; Muhammad is dead and therefore cannot fulfill this requirement. Jesus is not dead, even by the teaching of Muhammad which has Jesus in heaven in bodily form.

Surah 4:157-159 and Footnote 644, page 235-236:

"[157] That they said (in boast),

'We killed Christ Jesus

The son of Mary,

The Messenger of Allah' '—

But they killed him not,

Nor crucified him, [663]

But so it was made

To appear to them,

And those who differ

Therein are full of doubts,

With no (certain) knowledge,

But only conjecture to follow,

For of a surety They killed him not—

[158] Nay, Allah raised him up [664]

Unto Himself; and Allah

Is Exalted in Power, Wise—

[159] And there is none

Of the People of the Book

But must believe in him

Before his death; [665]

And on the Day of Judgment

He will be a witness [666]

Against them—."

Footnote 664

"Jews did not kill Jesus, but Allah raised him up to Himself. One school holds that Jesus did not die the usual human death, but still lives in the body in heaven, which is the generally, accepted Muslim view."

Second: John 14:26 clearly identifies the Holy Ghost as the comforter, and removes the "Comforter" from the fleshly and physical realm to the spiritual. Islam simply rejects any scripture verse that does not support its teaching, and selectively picks out those that do. If Muslims cannot find one that serves their purpose, they modify one and apply it instead.

These quotations from the Quran help reveal, the intent of satanic involvement in the Quran. With satanic guidance Muhammad sets forth a plan to remove Isaac from the Abrahamic covenant and replaces him with Ishmael. Satan's guidance is diverting the world away from Gods eternal purpose of life onto a path of death. If Muhammad had really understood the total plan of God from before creation to the final judgment, he would not have been deceived so easily.

Before the foundation of the world, God and Jesus together, developed a plan that would bring to an end all sin and evil once and for all. This plan included creation as we know it. This plan has at its core Jesus as Christ, the Abrahamic covenant through the lineage of Isaac, by Sarah, through King David to Jesus. This satanic deception not only removed the lineage of Isaac but removes Jesus from the throne of David and his birthright as the only begotten son of God and through atonement, the savior of the world.

By the time of the Hegira [flight] Muhammad was fully under the control of Satan. Through satanic guidance Muhammad has sown the seeds of deception. His plan is aimed at Jews and Christians and lays the foundation needed to set him up as the only answer to all spiritual matters.

Chapter Six

Muhammad's Gabriel

A great contradiction exists between the Archangel Gabriel of the Hebrew Bible (Old Testament), New Testament and the Gabriel of Mohammad's Quran. One important point must be established, there is only *one* Archangel Gabriel. When a comparison of the two Gabriel's is made, it becomes clear that the Gabriel Muhammad listened to was not the same Gabriel speaking in the Holy Bible. The first contradiction is seen in the actions of the two Gabriel's when they first appear. Within the Holy Bible, Gabriel, upon his appearance, would declare fear not and dispelled any fear of him. He never physically touched anyone except to strengthen them. In contrast Islamic tradition reports that when Muhammad first encountered the Archangel Gabriel, the archangel chocked him [Muhammad] four times which brought terror upon Muhammad.

Even though Gabriel was to have been the medium of communication between God and Muhammad, Muhammad questioned the experience. After his first experience with the Gabriel he met, Muhammad believed he was under the influence of an evil spirit. He expressed the fear and despair that came upon him to his wife Khadija. His doubts were so severe that he contemplated suicide. His wife Khadija, compared Muhammad's experience with the Gabriel he met to that of Moses and his first experience with God. In doing so she convinced him it was an angel who spoke to him and not the devil. However, when you compare the two experiences, there is no resemblance.

Richard Suskino, in his book *The Sword of the Prophet* quoted Muhammad's description of his first encounter with Gabriel as follows:

"The Archangel Gabriel came to me," he said later," With a cloth of brocade on which something was written, and said to me: 'Recite!' I answered: 'I cannot recite!' [For Muhammad could neither read nor write.] So Gabriel choked me with the cloth until I thought I was going to die. Then he released me and said again: 'Recite!' Again I replied that I could not recite, and again he chocked me." This happened four times, and finally Muhammad asked: "What shall I recite?" "I awoke in terror from my sleep."

The book of Exodus records Moses first encounter with God as follows and reveals no violent physical attack upon Moses:

Exodus 3:2-10

[2] And the angel of the LORD appeared unto him in a flame of fire out of the midst of a bush: and he looked, and, behold, the bush burned with fire, and the bush *was* not consumed.

[3] And Moses said, I will now turn aside, and see this great sight, why the bush is not burnt.

[4] And when the LORD saw that he turned aside to see, God called unto him out of the midst of the bush, and said, Moses, Moses. And he said, Here *am* I.

[5] And he said, Draw not nigh hither: put off thy shoes from off thy feet, for the place whereon thou standest *is* holy ground.

[6] Moreover he said, I *am* the God of thy father, the God of Abraham, the God of Isaac, and the God of Jacob. And Moses hid his face; for he was afraid to look upon God.

[7] And the LORD said, I have surely seen the affliction of my people which *are* in Egypt,

and have heard their cry by reason of their taskmasters; for I know their sorrows;

Muhammad believed that the Devil (Satan) had appeared to him and that he was under the influence of this evil spirit. A reasonable question to ask is what would be the motivating factor behind Satan impersonating the Archangel Gabriel? What would Satan gain? Could it be that in perpetuating this deception, Satan believed he could prevent the judgment day for himself? This is a point we will examine in detail later. Muhammad's Gabriel gave prophesies that are contradictory to prophesies given by Gabriel in the Holy Bible.

The Archangel Gabriel, of the Holy Bible prophesied many things, all of which have come to pass. The Gabriel of the Quran has prophesied many things, none of which have come to pass. Prophesies of Muhammad's Gabriel were a direct contradiction to the ones delivered to Daniel and Mary.

In Surah 59:13-14, Muhammad says Gabriel prophesied that the Jews would never unite and fight an Islamic army because they were more afraid of them than God. In addition he said the Jews were devoid of understanding and wisdom.

Surah 59: 13-14 pages 1446-1447:

"[13] Of a truth ye are
More feared
In their hearts,
Than Allah.[5389]
This is because they are
Men devoid of Understanding.

[14] They will not fight you
(Even) together, except
In fortified townships,
Or from behind walls,[5390]
Strong is their fighting (spirit)
Amongst themselves:
Thou wouldst think
They were united,
But their hearts are divided:[5391]
That is because they
Are a people devoid
Of Wisdom".

Nevertheless, in the last century Israel has engaged in no less than, five wars against Islamic armies and won them all. In addition, Jews have demonstrated some of the most brilliant minds of the modern world. It was a Jew who invented the atomic bomb. It was a Jew who invented television, not to mention being counselors and advisors to Kings and Presidents.

In Surah 5:41 The Muslim Gabriel said that the Jews were cursed in this world and the next.

Surah 5:41 Pages 259-260:

"O Messenger! Let not
Those grieve thee, who race
Each other into Unbelief:[744]
(Whether it be) among those
Who say " We believe"
With their lips but
Whose hearts have no faith;
Or it be among the Jews—
Men who will listen
To any lie—will listen
Even to others who have
Never so much as come[745]
To thee. They change the words
From their (right) times[746]
And place: they say
"If ye are given this,
Take it, but if not,
Beware!" If anyone's trial

Is intended by Allah, thou hast

No authority in the least

For him against Allah.

For such—is it not

Allah's will to purify

Their hearts. For them

There is disgrace

In this world, and

In the Hereafter

A heavy punishment."

This is a direct contradiction to *Daniel 9:21-24.*

Daniel 9:21-24 [21] "Yea, whiles I was speaking in prayer, even the man Gabriel, whom I had seen in the vision at the beginning, being caused to fly swiftly, touched me about the time of the evening oblation. [22] And he informed me, and talked with me, and said, O Daniel, I am now come forth to give thee skill and understanding. [23] At the beginning of thy supplications the commandment came forth, and I am come to shew thee; for thou art greatly beloved: therefore understand the matter, and consider the vision. [24] Seventy weeks are determined upon thy people and upon thy holy city, to finish the transgression, and to make an end of sins, and to make reconciliation for iniquity, and to bring in everlasting righteousness, and to seal up the vision and prophecy, and to anoint the most Holy."

In Surah 4:157 Mohammed's Gabriel proclaimed that Jesus did not die on the cross.

Surah 4:157 pages 235-236:

"That they said (in boast),
"We killed Christ Jesus
The son of Mary,
The Messenger of Allah"—
But they killed him not,
Nor crucified him,[663]
But so it was made
To appear to them.
And those who differ
Therein are full of doubts,
With no (certain) knowledge,
But only conjecture to follow,
For of a surety
They killed him not—"

This again contradicts what Gabriel told Daniel in Daniel 9:26

> *Daniel 9:26* "And after threescore and two weeks shall Messiah be cut off, but not for himself: and the people of the prince that shall come shall destroy the city and the sanctuary; and the end thereof shall be with a flood, and unto the end of the war desolations are determined."

The word "cut" here is the Hebrew word Karath; Kawraith; a prim. root; to cut (off, down or asunder); by implying to destroy or consume; specifically to covenant (i. e. make an alliance or bargain, originally by cutting flesh and passing between the pieces): This is the same type of blood covenant God made with Abraham concerning a seed (descendant), to which Muslims lay claim.

Now read and listen to the words of hate that comes from Mohammed's Gabriel and Muslim leaders, for those who believe that Jesus made a blood sacrifice with his own blood for our redemption. Undoubtedly, this is *not* the same Gabriel who prophesied Jesus, Son of God, to Mary.

Surah 19: 88-94 page 762

"⁸⁸ They say: "(Allah) Most Gracious
Has begotten a son!"

⁸⁹ Indeed ye have put forth
A thing most Monstrous: ²⁵²⁹

Footnote 2529

> "The belief in Allah begetting a son is not a
> question of words or of speculative thought.
> It is a stupendous blasphemy against Allah. It
> lowers Allah to the level of an animal. If com-
> bined with the doctrine of vicarious atonement,
> it amounts to a negation of Allah's justice and
> man's personal responsibility. It is destructive
> of all moral order and spiritual order, and is
> condemned in the strongest possible terms"

⁹⁰ As if the skies are ready
To burst, the earth
To split asunder, and
The mountains to fall down
In utter ruin.

⁹¹ That they should invoke
A son for (Allah) most Gracious.

[92] For it is not consonant

With the majesty of (Allah)

Most Gracious that He

Should beget a son. [2530]

[93] Not one of the beings

In the heavens and the earth

But must come to (Allah)

Most Gracious as a servant.

[94] He does take an account

Of them (all) and hath

Numbered them (all) exactly. [2531]"

Footnote 2531:

> Allah has no sons or favorites or parasites, such as we associate with human beings. On the other hand every creature of His gets His love, and His cherishing care. Every one of them, however humble, is individually marked before His Throne of Justice and Mercy, and will stand before Him on his own deserts.

In other words we have no need of a savior. Only our good works is needed to save us from the judgment day. Not just any good works, only the works of the Quran and nowhere else.

What Gabriel told Mary:

Luke 1:26-35 "[26] And in the sixth month the angel Gabriel was sent from God unto a city of Galilee, named Nazareth,[27] To a virgin espoused to a man whose name was Joseph, of the house of David; and the virgins name was Mary.[28] And the angel came in unto her, and said, Hail, thou that art highly favored, the Lord is with thee: blessed art thou among women.[29] And when she saw him, she was troubled at his saying, and cast in her mind what manner of salutation this should be.[30] And the angel said unto her, Fear not, Mary: for thou hast found favor with God.[31] And, behold, thou shalt conceive in thy womb, and bring forth a son, and shalt call his name JESUS.[32] He shall be great, and shall be called the Son of the Highest; and the Lord God shall give unto him the throne of his father David:[33] And he shall reign over the house of Jacob for ever; and of his kingdom there shall be no end.[34] Then said Mary unto the angel, How shall this be, seeing I know not a man?[35] And the angel answered and said unto her, The Holy Ghost shall come upon thee, and the power of the Highest shall overshadow thee: therefore also that holy thing which shall be born of thee shall be called the Son of God."

The point in all this is that there is only one being in all of God's creation that could hold such venomous anger directed at Jesus and His being the Son of God and that is Satan. For the birth of Jesus the Christ, Jesus the Son of God, marked the end of Satan's rule and insured his death in the lake of fire. Satan's hatred of Jesus has no bounds and since Jesus is now seated at the right hand of God. Satanic hatred is directed at mankind, the object of the love of Christ.

Romans 8:34
[34] Who *is* he that condemneth? *It is* Christ that died, yea rather, that is risen again, who is even at the right hand of God, who also maketh intercession for us.

Chapter Seven

The Satanic Plan Through Mohammed

With a plan in place that deals with the Christians and Jews, Muhammad now needed to find a way to appease the peoples of Mecca and his tribe the Quraish. A closer examination of Mohammed's method of dealing with Mecca, reveals hidden motives that guides his actions. First of all, the financial future of Mecca must be protected and Muhammad made sure his tribe the Quraish, would remain in power. When Muhammad overthrew Mecca he cast out of the Kaaba its multitude of idols and stone fetishes, but the temple itself, together with the Black Stone, was preserved as the supreme center of Islam, the holy place or "Mecca" to which each devout Muslim should make a pilgrimage. This appeased all Meccans, especially his family, the Quraish. For this decision kept his family in power and money within Mecca. *Surah 106:1-4 and footnote 6276, page 1702:*

"¹ For the covenants
(Of security and safeguard

75

Enjoyed) by the Qurash, [6276]

²Their covenants (covering) journeys
By winter and summer—[6277]

³ Let them adore the Lord
Of this House, [6278]

⁴ Who provides them
With food against hunger, [6279]
And with security
Against fear (of danger). [6280]"

Footnote 6276

"The Quraysh were the noblest tribe of Arabia, the tribe to which belonged the Holy Prophet himself. They had the custody of the Kabah, the central shrine of Arabia, and their possession of Mekkah gave them a triple advantage: (1) they had a commanding influence over the tribes; (2) their central position facilitated trade and intercourse, which gave them both honor and profit; and (3) the Makkah territory being, by Arabian custom, inviolable from the ravages of war and private feuds, they had a secure position, free from fear of danger. This honour and advantage they owed to their position as servants of the sacred shrine of the Kabah. They owed it to Allah. Was it not therefore right and fitting that they should adore the One True God, and listen to His Message of Unity and Purity, brought by His Prophet."

In those days of general insecurity, their prestige as custodians of Makkah (Mecca) and the Kaaba, enabled them to obtain covenants of security and safeguard from the rulers of neighboring countries on all sides – Syria, Persia, Yemen, and Abyssinia – protecting their trade journeys in all seasons."

As a point of information: the following are quotes from; *"Islam, Its Prophet, Peoples, Politics and Power,"* By George W. Braswell, Jr. Mr. Braswell taught at the Faculty of Islamic Theology of the University of Teheran from 1968 until 1974.

Page 14: "Most Meccans rejected Muhammad's message when he attacked the idols housed in the Ka'ba. They considered his preachments an economic threat to the commercial traders who visited the Ka'ba and a cultural threat to their way of life."

"Others offered to make him king when he later stated that he would allow the pagan dieties al-Lut, al-Uzza and al-Manat a place in his religion."

Page 44: "Before Islam there was no highly organized religion among the Arabs. Arabs recognized many gods and goddesses. Tribes had their own deities. There were astral deities. Arab Bedouins focused on the moon because it provided light during the night for their grazing flocks. Contemporary Islam also focused on the moon, as indicated by a crescent atop the mosque, a lunar calendar, and with festivals like Ramadan regulated by the rising of the moon."

"Pre-Islamic Arabia also had its stone deities. They were stone statues or shapeless volcanic or meteoric stones found in the deserts and believed to have been sent by astral deities. The most prominent deities were Hubal, the male god of the Ka'ba, and the three sister goddesses al-Lat, al-Manat, and al-Uzza; Muhammad's tribe, Quraysh, thought these three goddesses to be the daughters of Allah. Hubal was the chief god of the Ka'ba among 360 other deities. He was a man-like statue whose body was made of red precious stone and whose arms were of solid gold."

"Al-lat (with the t added to Allah) is the feminine form of Allah. She was represented by a square stone, and her major sanctuary was the city of Taif. Some thought of her as the female counterpart of Allah. Al-Manat was the goddess of fate whose major sanctuary consisted of a black stone in the town of Quadayd between Mecca and Medina."

"Al-Uzza was the goddess of east Mecca and was the most venerated deity of the Quraish tribe. It is said that human sacrifices were made to her. Islamic tradition reports that Muhammad's grandfather almost sacrificed his son, the father of Muhammad, to al-Uzza in fulfillment of a vow. However, he was counseled by a fortune teller to ransom his son with one hundred camels. Muslims interpret this as the will of Allah to bring Muhammad into existence."

Page 44-45 "Other deities in the Arabian peninsula included al-Rahman and al-Hajar, al-Aswad. Al-Rahman was the name of the ancient deity of southern Arabia. Muhammad used the name of this deity, which means "merciful," 169 times in the Quran. With the exception of Allah, it appears in the Quran more than any other descriptive term for Allah. All-Hajar, al-Aswad is symbolized by a black stone in the southeast corner of the Ka'ba. The stone was purportedly received by Ishmael from the angel Gabriel. Muhammad included it in the pilgrimage rituals in Mecca, and Muslims on the pilgrimage kiss the black stone in veneration."

The Islamic religion was supposed to be revealed to Muhammad by the Archangel Gabriel. How is it that God's Archangel Gabriel was going to accept idolatry into the true religion of Islam? It is clear that Muhammad wanted to include idol worship, and one which included human sacrifices (al-Uzza) as part of that worship. In addition, even the black stone Muslims kiss in respect to God, is in fact the product of idolatry, and violates the first of the Ten

Commandments. Muhammad's inclination to bargain away the principles of God extended to the Jews as well as his own family. The following is an additional quote from page 15 of Mr. Braswell's book.

> While at Medina —"Not only was there turmoil between Jewish and Arab tribes, but there also developed distrust between the emigrants (Muhajirun) from Mecca and the native helpers (Ansar) in Medina. Muhammad attempted to attract the Jews to his leadership. Some accepted him as prophet, but most became hostile to him."

> "In order to appease the Jews, Muhammad offered Friday as a beginning of the sabbath and the city of Jerusalem as the direction for prayer. When this effort failed. Muhammad selected Mecca toward which to pray and changed the Day of Atonement observed into the month-long fasting season of Ramadan."

> *NOTE:* All the above being so, how did Muhammad expect to sell the idea of human sacrifices and idolatry, not to mankind but, to God?

Mecca

Prior to Muhammad, Mecca was an important holy place and possessed the Kaaba [the cube], a square temple of uncut stones which contained the sacred Black Stone, by legend brought to Abraham and his son Ishmael by Gabriel. The stone had once been white, according to the tradition, the sins of those who touched it had changed it to black. The Kaaba housed the images of some three hundred sixty deities and fetishes [material objects believed to be the dwelling places of spirits capable of protecting the worshipers from harm and disease]. Credence was also given to the existence of a vague and little understood deity who was the ruler of the universe. He was called Allah-Taala [God-Almighty], but he did not figure actively in the popular religion, because he was not supposed to be particularly interested in human affairs. He [Muhammad] has now added to his new religion a god from each faith, Hebrew, Christian, and Pagan Idolatry to make his new idea palatable.

Muhammad has created a religion that caters to the dissentient, the wealthy and uncertain peoples of each faith, and those who--just like to fight and kill. It provides an easy path into paradise with little or no individual responsibility and has something for everyone. All of which advanced the spread of Islam. Mohammed's promised that any Muslim dying in battle for the faith was assured entrance into paradise. In addition, Muhammad promised his followers would have dominion if they should carry Islam to the end of the earth.

One last thing, Muhammad incorporated a policy used by Alexander the Great which included local customs into his government. This kept the local people from rebelling. In addition he encouraged his leaders, men only, to marry into the local population. This worked very well to the advantage of Muhammad, who needed the local money to finance his new religion. For Christian and Jews, if they submitted to the new rule, would be allowed to pursue their former way of living and retain their own religion, as long as they paid a tax. All in all, Mohammed's new religion prays on the fear of the people. He has taken the truth and mingled it with the false and produced a deception the world could believe.

The worst kind of a lie is one that has an element of truth in it. Here the teachers of Islam have taken true facts and distorted them to fit their political agenda. There is an obvious attempt to corrupt the law of God and incorporate the idolatry of the Mecca thereby deceiving the people into belief in Muhammad's new god, a false god.

The Sunna

There are two fundamental sources of Islamic doctrine and practice, the Quran and Sunna. The Sunna is a book chronicling the exemplary conduct of the prophet. The teaching of Islam proclaims that Muhammad was considered infallible. Notwithstanding, the Quran allows a man to have four wives. After Khadija's death Muhammad took nine wives and one of them was Asha, his cousin. Quoting Mr. Braswell,

"She was six years old when they were married, though he did not consummate the Marriage until she was nine."

This marriage, and Muhammad's consummation, with a nine year old, identifies Muhammad as a child molester, in his time and ours. Along with his nine wives he had a Christian Coptic slave as a concubine. All of which violates the Old Testament Ten Commandments which are, conveniently, not mentioned in the Quran. Among the teachings of the Quran, Muslims are not to lie, cheat, stealing or commit murder. Here, when proclaiming Mohammed's infallibility, Muslims conveniently leave out Muhammad's caravan raids while he lived in Medina and the adultery after the death of Khadija, and the massacre of the Jews in Medina. Once again

Islamic teachers have taken a true fact and twisted it into a deception.

Recent research, not yet accepted by the large body of Muslims, has demonstrated that much of the Sunna was not derived from Muhammad but represents the opinions of the early generations of Muslims. In some cases a genuine statement of the prophet was preserved, but additions to it were later made by Muslims who wanted to advance certain theological or legal opinions.

The truth mingled with a lie is a very deceiving thing and the greatest tool of Satan. First, he takes a truth, creates a doubt by introducing a lie with just the right amount of truth to make it believable. The satanic influence on Muhammad is clear and Satan's mark unmistakable.

Chapter Eight
Contradictions within the Quran

Muhammad has now cast a shadow of doubt over the Jewish Bible, claiming it to be corrupted, by the Jews. Along with denouncing Jesus as the Lord, Messiah and the Son of God, and incorporating a piece of culture from Alexander the Great. To complete the mix he included some of the pre-Islamic paganism of Mecca. His religion now appeases his family and keeps them in money and power. Muhammad begins to establish himself as the sole "light" and answer to all faiths.

As you read the Quran, you will find constant referrals to the Hebrew Bible and Jesus. However, they are used only in the context of establishing Muhammad as the single answer to all things. All references from the Hebrew Bible and Jesus are not direct quotes but paraphrased versions of Mohammed, supposedly given to him by Gabriel. In most cases they are out right distortions. Amazing is it not, the Hebrew Bible and Jesus, corrupted as Muhammad proclaims, remain the major sources for verifying his claim as the "Seal of the Prophets."

It is now important to establish the true validity of the "corrupted" Hebrew Bible to Muhammad. To support my thesis I will use the Quran itself. If I were to use another book, Muslims would reject the proofs submitted. Muhammad and Muslims in general extract those things from the Hebrew Bible, which they believe will support their teachings and denounce the rest as corrupted by Israel.

Once again we have a contradiction in the teaching. First, we are told the Hebrew Bible and New Testament are corrupted, yet the Quran in C55 and Surah 3:23 and footnotes 366 page 132, says that the Hebrew Bible and the New Testament of Jesus are to be combined with the Quran to make the "whole book of Allah".

C 55, Page 131:

"If the people who received
Earlier revelations confine themselves
To partial truths, and in their pride
Shut their eyes to the whole of the Book
Of Allah, their day is done;
Let the Muslims seek the society
And friendship of their own, and trust
In Allah, who knows all, and holds
Every soul responsible for its own deeds."

Surah 3:23, page 132:

"Hast thou not turned
Thy vision to those
Who have been given a portion [366]
Of the Book? They are
Invited to the Book of Allah,
To settle their dispute,
But a party of them
Turn Back and decline (The arbitration).[367]"

Footnote 366:

"A portion of the Book. I conceive that Allah's revelation as a whole throughout the ages is "The Book". The Law of Moses, and the Gospel of Jesus were portions of the Book. The Quran completes the revelation and is par excellence the Book of Allah."

Also Surah 2:136 page 55, mandates belief in Abraham, Isaac, Jacob, Ishmael, Moses, Jesus and (all) prophets of the Lord.

Surah 2:136 pages 55-56:

"Say ye: "We believe in Allah, and
The revelation given to us, and
To Abraham, Ismail, Isaac, Jacob,
And the descendants (children
Of Jacob) and that given to
Moses and Jesus and that given
To (all) Prophets from their Lord:
We make no difference
Between one and another of them:
And we bow to Allah (in Islam)".

NOTE: Muhammad taught that all prophets of
all religions were from God. Buddhist, Hindu
etc. and we must listen to all of them.

In Surah 19:54 and footnote 2506, Ishmael is proclaimed the sacrifice of Abraham, not Isaac. Here is another contradiction where Ishmael is substituted for Isaac. This proclamation conveniently ignores one of the basic elements of the covenant God made with Abraham. In this case Sarah his wife was to be the mother of the seed, not Hagar.

Surah 19:54, page 755:

"Also mention in the Book
(The story of) Ismail:
He was (strictly) true
To what he promised, [2506]
And he was a messenger
(And) a prophet."

Footnote 2506:

"Ismail was Dhabih, Alliah, i.e., the chosen sacrifice of Allah in Muslim traditions. When Abraham told him of the sacrifice, he voluntarily offered himself for it, and never flinched from his promise, until the sacrifice was redeemed by the substitution of a ram under Allah's commands. He was the fountainhead of the Arabian Ummah, and in his posterity came the Prophet of Allah. The Ummah and the Book of Islam reflect back the prophethood on Ismail."

The book of Genesis does speak of Ishmael and proclaimed a promise from God that he would be the father of a great nation. However, that nation would be a nation in size, not honor. Ishmael was to be a warring man. His hand was to be against every man and every man's hand would be against him.

Genesis 16:11-12

[11] And the angel of the LORD said unto her, Behold, thou *art* with child, and shalt bear a son, and shalt call his name Ishmael; because the LORD hath heard thy affliction.
[12] And he will be a wild man; his hand *will be* against every man, and every man's hand against him; and he shall dwell in the presence of all his brethren.

So this is the posterity of Ishmael that has been passed on to his great nation, the warring attitude of Islam.

In addition, Muhammad in Surah 4:157-159 and footnote 664 says that Jesus was not killed by the Jews that God raised him up. Not because he was the Messiah or the son of God, but because he was a perfect prophet. Muslims believe that Jesus did not die the usual human death, but still lives in the body in heaven.

Surah 4:157-159, page 235-236:

"[157] That they said (in boast),

"We have killed Christ Jesus
The son of Mary,
The Messenger of Allah'—
But they killed him not,
Nor crucified him, [663]
But so it was made
To appear to them,
And those who differ
Therein are full of doubts,
With no (certain) knowledge,
But only conjecture to follow,
For of a surety
They killed him not.

[158] Nay, Allah raised him up [644]
Unto Himself; and Allah
Is Exalted in Power, Wise—

[159] And there is none
Of the People of the Book
But must believe in him
Before his death; [655]
And on the Day of Judgment
He will be a witness [666]
Against them—"

Footnote 664:

"There is a difference of opinions as to the exact interpretation of this verse. The words are: The Jews did not kill Jesus, but Allah raised him up (rafa'ahu) to Himself. One school holds that Jesus did not die the usual human death, but still lives in the body in heaven, which is the generally accepted Muslim view. Another holds that he did die (5:120) but not when he was supposed to be crucified, and that his being 'raised up' unto Allah means that instead of being disgraced as a malefactor, as the Jews intended, he was on the contrary honoured by Allah as His Messenger: (see 4:159). The same word rafa'a is used in association with honour in connection with al Mustafa in 94:4."

NOTE: Notice that here three different verses are cited all with a different idea of what happened to Jesus. One common thread is that he was not sacrificed for the world's sins. Muhammad's Gabriel did not have a definite answer on the status of Jesus. How could this be as Gabriel is an Archangel who serves in the presence of God? The Holy Bible affirms that Jesus is sitting on the right hand of God in view of the archangels. The question now arises, with Muhammad's superseding of Jesus, why would Gabriel not have made it clear the status of Jesus? Satanic deception seeks to remove Jesus our savior.

In accepting Mohammed's proclamation concerning the perfect life of Jesus. We must accept the prophets acknowledgment that Jesus told "no" lies. Therefore, one would reason that, Muslims must accept the statements of Jesus in *Luke 24:44,* but they do not.

> [44] "And he said unto them, These are the words which I spake unto you, while I was yet with you, that all things must be fulfilled, which were written in the law of Moses, and in the prophets, and in the psalms, concerning me."

Clearly, Jesus endorses the Old Testament used in His day as the true, word of God. He in no way declares it to be the corrupted word that Muhammad and Muslims claims it to be. Now, as we, proceed through the Quran we find a great number of verses that not only contradict the Old and New Testaments, but contradict the Quran itself. For example, The

Old Testament "Torah" says God created man from the dust of the ground, *Genesis 2:7.*

> [7] "And the Lord God formed man of the dust of the ground, and breathed into his nostrils the breath of life; and man became a living soul."

The Quran both agrees with and contradicts it.

Surah 96:1-2 page 1672,

"[1]Proclaim! (or Read!)
In the name
Of thy Lord and Cherisher,
Who created—
[2] Created man, out of
A (mere) clot
Of congealed blood.

Surah 19:67 page 758,

"But does not man
Call to mind that We
Created him before
Out of nothins?"

Surah 35:11 page 1104,

"And Allah did create
You from dust:
Then from a sperm drop;…"

Surah 38:71 page 1176,

"Behold, thy Lord said
To the angels: I am
About to create man
From clay:"

Surah 40:67 page 1223,

"It is He Who has
Created you from dust
Then from a sperm-drop,
Then from a leech-like clot;…"

There are more verses that use blood clot and some use semen. My point is, there is no consistency within the Quran on this point. Which is it, was man created from dust, clay, sticky clay, semen or a clot of congealed blood? If we were created from a "sperm drop," there is a question of who's was it. Please remember I am using only the scriptures that

Muhammad has certified as the true word of God and quotes from Jesus, whom Muhammad has proclaimed a perfect prophet:

Surah 112:3 page 1714 and footnote 6299; clearly states that God did not and has not begotten a son.

³ "He begetteh not, Nor is he begotten,"6299
Referring to God. *Footnote 6299* says

"This is the negative of the Christian idea of the godhead, The Father, the only begotten Son, etc."

Notwithstanding, Jesus on many occasions said God was his father.

John 1:18 No "man hath seen God at any time; the only begotten Son, which is in the bosom of the Father, he hath declared him."

John 3:16 "For God so loved the world, that he gave his only begotten Son, that whosoever believeth in him should not perish, but have everlasting life."

John 3:18 "He that believeth on him is not condemned: but he that believeth not is condemned already, because he hath not believed in the name of the only begotten Son of God."

Furthermore, Jesus has put forth two requirements that each individual must pass through to become part of the kingdom of God. John 3:3 and 3:5:

John 3:3 "Jesus answered and said unto him, Verily, verily, I say unto thee, Except a man be born again, he cannot see the kingdom of God."

John 3:5 "Jesus answered, Verily, verily, I say unto thee, Except a man be born of water and of the Spirit, he cannot enter into the kingdom of God."

In verse three a requirement of a new birth is needed just to "see" the kingdom. In verse five one must be born a third time to enter the kingdom. Three separate and distinct births are required for entering the Kingdom of God. First is our natural birth that all mankind comes through. The second is our first step into the spiritual world where we can see the kingdom. Third, is the birth through baptism of water and spirit for us to enter into the Kingdom. Everyone is blessed with our physical birth. As we pass through this life we are required to make a decision concerning God and Jesus. We can accept them and their teachings or reject them. John 3:18 makes it clear that those who refuse belief in Jesus have sealed their fate, and stand condemned before God. Satan had deceived Muhammad into falling in this trap and Muhammad leads Muslims into the same trap.

> *John 3:18* "He that believeth on him is not condemned: but he that believeth not is condemned already, because he hath not believed in the name of the only begotten Son of God."

The following are more examples of Satanic distortions.

Surah 2:31 page 24

"And He taught Adam the name
Of all things; then he placed them
Before the angels, and said "Tell Me
The names of these if ye are right."

> *Genesis 2:18-19* "[18] And the Lord God said, It is not good that the man should be alone; I will make him an help meet for him. [19] And out of

the ground the Lord God formed *every beast of the field,* and every fowl of the air; and brought them unto Adam to see what he would call them: and *whatsoever Adam called every living creature, that was the name thereof."*

Genesis 3:1 "NOW the serpent was more subtil than any beast of the field which the Lord God had made. And he said unto the woman, Yea, hath God said, Ye shall not eat of every tree of the garden?"

NOTE: Satan has disguised himself as an angel of light and does not want the world to see that he is nothing more than one of the beasts of the field. We will look into this in more detail later.

2 Corinthians 11:14
[14] And no marvel; for Satan himself is transformed into an angel of light.

Surah 2:34 page 25

"And behold, we said to the angels; "Bow down to Adam," and they bowed down…"

Hebrews 1:5-6 [5] "For to which of the angels did He ever say: "You are My Son, Today I have begotten You"? And again: "I will be to Him a Father, And He shall be to Me a Son"? [6] But when He again brings the firstborn into the world, He says: "Let all the angels of God worship Him.""

Psalms 89:26 "He shall cry unto me, Thou art my father, my God, and the rock of my salvation"

Surah 2:31 and 2:34 are clear and outright distortions and lies. There is no recorded commandment from God for angels to worship Adam. However, the book of Hebrews quoted above, God clearly commands *the angels to worship Jesus.*

Chapter Nine
The Holy Bible

At this point it is important that the validity of the Holy Bible be established. It is equally important to establish why Christians hold the Holy Bible as the only true and final word of God. Therefore, this chapter is devoted to the cannon of the Holy Bible. It will be needed to understand the next chapter, The Satanic Deception.

In Deuteronomy, God made it very clear that we were not to add to or take away from the words he gave to Moses.

> *Deuteronomy 4:2* "Ye shall not add unto the word which I command you, neither shall ye diminish ought from it, that ye may keep the commandments of the Lord your God which I command you."

> *Deuteronomy 32:46-47* [46] "And he said unto them, Set your hearts unto all the words which I testify among you this day, which ye shall command your children to observe to do, all the words of this law. [47] For it is not a vain thing

for you; because it is your life: and through this thing ye shall prolong your days in the land, whither ye go over Jordan to possess it."

Based upon the above mentioned scriptures, an accurate decree, on the bounds of the canon are essential if we are to obey God. An accurate collection of writings that constitute God's words to us becomes central to our faith and practice. Which writings then constitute God's words to us, thereby, qualifying them, to occupy a place within our rules of faith and practice? To the Roman Catholic, all those books which the "church" had decided to be divine in their origin, and none others, are to be received. To Protestants, so far as the Old Testament is concerned, those books, and those only, which Christ and His Apostles recognized as the written word of God, are regarded as canonical. As you can see these statements alone produce a void between some of the participants.

To say that there have been heated debates about the canon of scripture would be the understatement of the year. Scholars and non-scholars have debated the validity of the scriptures from both sides of the issue. Those who wish to prove the truth and reality of the scriptures as the word of God, those who wish to discredit it. The dramatic irony of the situation is that each side uses the canon as the basis of their argument. This paper will deal with only one side of the debate, that which is in favor of the scriptures. Many of our leading scholars, in support of the canon, use external evidence to supplement and support the internal evidence of the scriptures. Nevertheless, for every Christian, the quandary begins with the word canon itself. What does "canon" mean?

The word canon came from the Greek word "kanon" which means a rod used for measuring as a rule. It is from here that the English word takes on other meanings such as standard or rule. When applied to the scriptures such terms as "canons of the church" becomes rules or standards of the church. Herein lays the origin of the debate within the church. Differences in opinion as to just what is and is not a standard that the church must follow has produced many denominations. This issue alone has effectively separated God's people into many different factions, who at times bitterly oppose one another. Nevertheless, there is no better place to find the true canons of God's word than within the scriptures themselves. Therefore, let us begin with the canonization of the Old Testament.

Old Testament Canon

There is very little debate, concerning the canon of the Old Testament, known as the Hebrew Bible, which is codified in the three fold divisions of the book, known as the TeNaKh.

The Te stands for the Torah, Hebrew for the law. This section is comprised of the first five books written by Moses; Genesis, Exodus, Leviticus, Numbers, and Deuteronomy. The Na stands for Nebiim, Hebrew for Prophets. This portion is comprised of two sections, the Former Prophets, Joshua, Judges, Samuel, Kings. The second section is the Latter Prophets, Isaiah, Jeremiah, Ezekiel, and the Book of the Twelve Prophets. The third division, the Kh, is known as the Kitbim or the writings. This section contains Psalms, Proverbs, and Job then a group of five books known as the Megillot or scrolls; they are the Song of Solomon, Ruth, Lamentations, Ecclesiastes, Ester and finally Daniel, Ezra-Nehemiah and Chronicles. There is a difference in the numbers of books when compared to the Holy Bible of the Christian era. This discrepancy is accounted for in that the Hebrew Bible counts some books as one, which is counted as two in the Christian Bible. No attempt will be made here to explain the differences. The Apocrypha was never included within or as a part of the Hebrew Bible by the Jews.

It would be negligent to fail in addressing the intentional omission of the Apocrypha from the protestant bible. The main point to be made here is, of the 295 references found in the New Testament a scripture quoting the Old Testament, not one reference is made to any of the books of the Apocrypha. However, there is no evidence within the New Testament of a dispute between Jesus and the Jews concerning the canon of the Old Testament. Additions to the Old Testament ceased after the times of Ezra, Nehemiah, Ester, Haggai, Zachariah, and Malachi. Suffice it to say, the Hebrew Bible known, to Protestant Christian believers, as the Old Testament is accepted as fully canonized.

New Testament Canon

The main dispute on canonization lies with the volumes of the New Testament. Even though the debate over canonization of the New Testament began in the early ages, and continues today, the best evidence for its validity is found within the Old Testament. One of the problems, in the present day debate, lies in the modern definition of the word "testament" which is somewhat confusing. It implies a person's last will and testament, which takes effect upon the death of the testator. When the church asserts that Jesus has risen from the dead and remains alive there seems to exist a conflict of definitions. However, the Greek word or testament is Diatkeke which, can refer to a will, but is more commonly used in various kinds of settlements in which one party is superior to another. It places privileges on the inferior and certain obligations on the superior. The present day word "covenant" would be more useful word in place of Testament. With this definition in mind it is easy to understand why the Old Testament, which dealt with the Abrahamic Covenant, was so readily canonized.

Now that the Old Testament was accepted as canon, canonization of the New Testament would then mandate conformity and harmony with the Old Testament. This principle is supported by the words of Jesus in *Luke 24:44*

> *Luke 24:44* "And he said unto them, These are the words which I spake unto you, while I was yet with you, that all things must be fulfilled, which were written in the law of Moses, and in the prophets, and in the psalms, concerning me."

Our Lord makes it clear in this verse that all three divisions of the Old Testament, held as canon, speak directly of him. The bridge between the Old and New Testaments is confirmed in numerous places throughout the New Testament. In 1 Corinthians 10:11-12 the Apostle Paul refers to the teachings of the Old Testament as necessary for our admonition and training as concerning the end time happenings.

> [1] *Corinthians 10:11-12* [11] Now all these things happened unto them for ensamples: and they were written for our admonition, upon whom

the ends of the world are come. [12] Wherefore let him that thinketh he standeth take heed lest he fall"

When the Apostle Paul wrote to Timothy, 2 Timothy 3:16-17, he affirmed that the, known canonized scriptures in existence at that time, the Hebrew Bible, was to be used as the guide or rule for instruction in Godly living.

> [2] *Timothy 3:16-17* [16] "All scripture is given by inspiration of God, and is profitable for doctrine, for reproof, for correction, for instruction in righteousness: [17] That the man of God may be perfect, thoroughly furnished unto all good works."

Once again, at the time the Apostle Paul made this statement, the only scriptures in existence was the Old Testament. The authority of these scriptures has never been in question. However, a question that has evolved is who made them into a collection? This question does not inquire of God's part in the scriptures, but man's part. Just exactly how the Hebrews, of Old Testament times, viewed the concept of a canon, is not known. Nevertheless, it is safe to say that the idea existed long before anyone put a name on it. However, this argument, as strong as it is, does not completely answer the questions as to what writings are entitled to occupy a place within our rules of faith and practice and who made that decision.

The Rules

Five main rules set the standard for what could be included in the canon of the New Testament. First, the writings had to be authored by an apostle. The development of the canon began with the writings of the apostles, which concern God's great acts in redemptive history. It is primarily the apostles who are given the ability from the Holy Spirit to recall accurately the words and deeds of Jesus and to interpret them rightly for subsequent generations.

Because the apostles, by virtue of their apostolic office, had authority to write words of Scripture. The authentic written teachings of the apostles were accepted by the early church as part of the canon of Scripture. This would include Matthew; John, Romans to Philemon (all of the Pauline epistles); James; 1st and 2nd Peter; 1st, 2nd, and 3rd, John; and Revelation. This leaves five books, Mark, Luke, Acts, Hebrews and Jude, which were not written by apostles. This introduces the second qualifier for authorship of a canonized writing. The writer must be a close associate of an apostle. Mark with Peter, Luke with Paul, Jude apparently was accepted by virtue of his connection with James and the fact that he was the brother of Jesus. The author of Hebrews has been traditionally attributed to Paul. However, this idea has been rejected from very early times. Who actually authored Hebrews, God only knows. Its acceptance as canon is based more on its intrinsic qualities rather that authorship. Hebrews, fulfills the third requirement, that of edification when read in public.

The fourth and fifth requirements are that the writings must not be overly repetitious and that they must agree with present truth. Obviously, all of the New Testament books meet these standards.

Final List

In A.D. 367 the Thirty-Ninth Paschal Letter of Athanasius contained and exact list of the twenty-seven New Testament books we have today. This list of books was accepted by the churches in the eastern part of the Mediterranean world. Thirty years later, in A.D. 397, the Council of Carthage, representing the churches of the western part of the Mediterranean worlds, agreed with the eastern churches on the same list. These are the earliest final lists of our present-day canon.

The apostles and their close companions report Christ's words and deeds and interpret time with absolute divine authority. With this in mind a clear understanding of how the writer of Hebrews 1:1-2, proclaims why no more writings can be added to the Bible after the times of the New Testament. One fact is sure, the canon is closed.

Hebrews 1:1-2. [1] "God, who at sundry times and in divers manners spake in time past unto the fathers by the prophets. [2] Hath in these last days spoken unto us by *his* Son, whom he hath appointed heir of all things, by whom also he made the worlds;"

Conclusion

How do we know, then, that we have the right books in the canon of Scriptures, we now possess? The question can be answered tn two different ways. First, if we are asking upon what we should base our confidence; the answer must ultimately be that our confidence is based on the faithfulness of God. Secondly, we focus on the process by which we become persuaded that the books we have now in the canon are the right ones. In this process two factors are at work; the activity of the Holy Spirit convincing us as we read Scriptures for ourselves, and the historical information that we have available for our consideration. There is therefore historical confirmation for the correctness of the current canon. Yet it must be remembered in connection with any historical investigation that the work of the early church was not to bestow, divine authority or even ecclesiastical authority upon some merely human writings, but rather to recognize the divinely authored characteristic of writings that already had such quality. This is because the ultimate criterion of canonicity is divine authorship, not human or ecclesiastical approval

The evidence of canonization found within the scripture is without doubt more than sufficient to ratify itself. There is no other document on earth that has built within its covers thousands of years of accurate history, supported by archeology and confirmed by God, that can of itself, prove itself true. There is no better proof of validity for the scriptures than that of the scriptures themselves. The unity and harmony of scriptures, Old and New Testament, coupled with the witness of the only living God is quite sufficient to stand any scrutiny man can offer.

Chapter Ten

Why the Satanic Deception

For those outside of Christendom all of this is foolishness. The rejection of Islam will be obvious. However, for the followers of Christ, this satanic deception has a powerful effect upon their lives. Whether rejected or accepted, it is important that this veil of deceit be removed and the truth revealed for all to see. Why would Satan go to such lengths to perpetuate this deception? The answer is simple; Jesus the Christ, with his crucifixion and resurrection, defeated Satan and all his works and condemned Satan to the lake of fire. (Revelations 20:10) To fully understand this situation, past present and future, we must know who Satan is and where he came from. Why was this universe and world created? Why did it require the life, crucifixion and resurrection of Jesus to defeat Satan and his works? What then is the works of Satan and what is the goal he is working to obtain? Simply put, he [Satan] is working to save his own life, for he knows that the penalty of sin is death. Satan knows that God has put the judgment of this world and angles in the hands of the saints, 1Corinthians 6:2-3 and Daniel 7:22. If he can deceive the whole of humanity, who would be worthy enough to sit on the judgment seat against him?

1 Corinthians 6:2-3 "² Do ye not know that *the saints shall judge the world?* and if the world shall be judged by you, are ye unworthy to judge the smallest matters? ³ *Know ye not that we shall judge angels?* how much more things that pertain to this life?"

Daniel 7:22 "Until the Ancient of days came, and *judgment was given to the saints* of the most High; and the time came that the saints possessed the kingdom."

In the Book of Genesis Chapter 2 verses 15-17 it says this:

"¹⁵ And the Lord God took the man, and put him into the garden of Eden to dress it and to keep it. ¹⁶ And the Lord God commanded the man, saying, Of every tree of the garden thou mayest freely eat: ¹⁷ But of the tree of the knowledge of good and evil, thou shalt not eat of it: for in the day that thou eatest thereof thou shalt surely die."

Here God told Adam that in the day he ate of the tree of knowledge of good and evil that he, Adam, would die. There is a realization here of death existing in Adam's life before he ate of the tree. Adam understood death and so did Satan, who was in the Garden with him. However, Satan somehow was able to take hold of the tree of life and remain in heaven, while Adam was cast out to the earth.

Genesis 3:22-24

22 And the LORD God said, Behold, the man is become as one of us, to know good and evil: and now, lest he put forth his hand, and take also of the tree of life, and eat, and live for ever:

23 Therefore the LORD God sent him forth from the garden of Eden, to till the ground from whence he was taken.

24 So he drove out the man; and he placed at the east of the garden of Eden Cherubims, and a flaming sword which turned every way, to keep the way of the tree of life.

Nevertheless, Jesus came and made a way for Satan to be cast out from heaven and face the judgment for his sin. At the same time the sacrifice of Jesus made atonement for our sins.

The atoning blood of Jesus made us, through grace, worthy to sit in judgment of Satan.

Now, Satan's only hope of saving his life is to prevent the man child of Revelation 12 from being caught up to the Throne of God. Revelation 12:4 says that Satan is waiting to devour the man child. Even Peter in, 1 Peter 5:8, describes Satan as a roaring lion seeking whom he may devour, and Jesus, in John 8:44 characterized Satan as a lustful liar and murderer from his beginnings.

> [1] *Peter 5:8* "Be sober, be vigilant; because your adversary the devil, as a roaring lion, walketh about, seeking whom he may devour:

> *John 8:44* "Ye are of your father the devil, and the lusts of your father ye will do. He was a murderer from the beginning, and abode not in the truth, because there is no truth in him. When he speaketh a lie, he speaketh of his own: for he is a liar, and the father of it."

Knowing that we are living in the last days Satan's attention has shifted to a child who is to be born and caught up to the throne of God. When this occurs, Michael and his angels will cast Satan and all his followers out of heaven to face his judgment. This marks his imminent end.

Revelation 12:3-9 "³And there appeared another wonder in heaven; and behold a great red dragon, having seven heads and ten horns, and seven crowns upon his heads. ⁴ And his tail drew the third part of the stars of heaven, and did cast them to the earth: and the dragon stood before the woman which was ready to be delivered, *for to devour her child as soon as it was born.*⁵ And she brought forth a man child, who was to rule all nations with a rod of iron: and her child was caught up unto God, and to his throne. ⁶ And the woman fled into the wilderness, where she hath a place prepared of God, that they should feed her there a thousand two hundred and threescore days. ⁷ And there was war in heaven: Michael and his angels fought against the dragon; and the dragon fought and his angels, ⁸ And prevailed not; neither was their place found any more in heaven. ⁹ *And the great dragon was cast out, that old serpent, called the Devil, and Satan, which deceiveth the whole world: he was cast out into the earth, and his angels were cast out with him.*"

Satan believes he can devour this child before it can be caught up to the throne of God. The word "devour" used here means to consume or eat up. In other words absorb the world's population into Islam so the man child cannot be brought forth. In Matthew 24:22-24 Jesus describes the seriousness of these days this way: This is not a futile effort on Satan's part because, if God does not intervene, it has a chance of working.

> *Matthew 24:22-24* "[22]And except those days should be shortened, there should no flesh be saved: but for the elects sake those days shall be shortened.[23] Then if any man shall say unto you, Lo, here is Christ, or there; believe it not.[24] For there shall arise false Christs, and false prophets, and shall shew great signs and wonders; insomuch that, if it were possible, they shall deceive the very elect."

It is clear that Satan believes, that if he can change the rules of morality, which God has put in place, he can devour the man child and save his life. Therefore, if he can establish another faith [Islam] that does not require a Messiah, he can deceive even God's elect. Nevertheless, one thing is clear; Satan does not have the welfare of mankind at heart in fostering this deception. Even those who do not believe in God or Satan are not exempt.

All this means nothing to an atheist. They look upon Muslims, Jews and Christians as peoples who manipulate events to further their own ambitions. These three groups, for the most part, have a very simplistic view of Satan and his involvement in world affairs. As for me, satanic influences are one of the areas where my understanding has changed. Therefore, I intend to put forth, for your consideration, my view on the beginnings, the purpose and the end of Satan. In doing so, I will be able to expose the half truths, that Muhammad, and my own faith has taught about Satan. We will begin with his beginnings in Genesis 3. One must also ask why the origins of Satan are omitted from the Quran. Here we have the story of the events that led up to the fall of man from the Garden of Eden and the satanic involvement in Adams fall.

> *Genesis 3:1* "NOW the serpent was more subtil
> than any beast of the field which the Lord God
> had made. And he said unto the woman, Yea,
> hath God said, Ye shall not eat of every tree of
> the garden?"

I cannot remember of hearing the serpent beast mentioned here identified as anyone other than Satan. How do we identify this serpent beast with Satan? The answer is in Revelation 12:7-9 and 20:1-2:

> *Revelation 12:7-9* "7And there was war in heaven: Michael and his angels fought against the dragon; and the dragon fought and his angels,8 And prevailed not; neither was their place found any more in heaven.9 And the great dragon was cast out, *that old serpent, called the Devil, and Satan,* which deceiveth the whole world: he was cast out into the earth, and his angels were cast out with him."

> *Revelation 20:1* "¹ AND I saw an angel come down from heaven, having the key of the bottomless pit and a great chain in his hand.² And he laid *hold on the dragon, that old serpent, which is the Devil, and Satan,* and bound him a thousand years, ²And he laid hold on the dragon, that old serpent, which is the Devil, and Satan, and bound him a thousand years,"

Here in Revelation, John identifies the serpent as the Devil and Satan. I am using Revelation because John, the author, is one of the New Testament prophets that Muhammad uses to validate his [Muhammad's] ministry. Now, with the help of John we have identified the serpent of Genesis 3:1 as the Devil and Satan and that he was not an angel but one of the beasts of the field God had made. Now look at Genesis 2:15-25:

Genesis 2:15-25 "15 And the Lord God took the man, and put him into the garden of Eden to dress it and to keep it.16 And the Lord God commanded the man, saying, Of every tree of the garden thou mayest freely eat:17 But of the tree of the knowledge of good and evil, thou shalt not eat of it: for in the day that thou eatest thereof thou shalt surely die.18 And the Lord God said, It is not good that the man should be alone; I will make him an help meet for him.19 *And out of the ground the Lord God formed every beast of the field, and every fowl of the air; and brought them unto Adam to see what he would call them: and whatsoever Adam called every living creature, that was the name thereof.20 And Adam gave names to all cattle, and to the fowl of the air, and to every beast of the field;* but for Adam there was not found an help meet for him.21 And the Lord God caused a deep sleep to fall upon Adam, and he slept: and he took one of his ribs, and closed up the flesh instead thereof;²² And the rib, which the Lord God had taken from man, made he a woman, and brought her unto the man.²³ And Adam said, This is now bone of my bones, and flesh of my flesh: she shall be called Woman, because she was taken out of Man.²⁴ Therefore shall a man leave his father and his mother, and shall cleave unto his wife: and they shall be one flesh.²⁵ And they were both naked, the man and his wife, and were not ashamed."

Notice that, in verse 19, God formed the beasts of the field out of the ground in the Garden of Eden. After forming the beasts of the field, God brought them to Adam to see what Adam would call them. In verse 20 Adam gave the names to all the cattle, fowl and every beast of the field. It is obvious, from Genesis 3:1 and 2:15-25, that Satan was "not" an angel and that Adam was formed before Satan and in fact named Satan. We will deal with the so called "angelic status of Satan" later. It is important to know that, while impersonating the Archangel Gabriel, Satan goes to great length, in the Quran, hiding his true identity and origin. His first attempt is found in Surah 2.

NOTE: Names in the Bible are descriptions of the nature of the individual. For instance, Jacob means heal-catcher, (i.e., supplanter). God changed his name to Israel which means, he will rule as God.

Surah 2:31-33, page 24 contradicts Adam's naming of the beasts of the field:

Surah 2:31-33:

"31 And He taught Adam the names[48]
Of all things; then He placed them
Before the angels, and said: 'Tell Me
The names of these if ye are right.'

32 They said: 'Glory to Thee: of knowledge
We have none, save Thou
Hast taught us. In truth it is Thou
Who art perfect in knowledge and wisdom.'

33 He said: 'O Adam! Tell them
Their names.' When he had told them,
Allah said: 'Did I not tell you
That I know the secrets of heaven
And earth, and I know what ye reveal

And what ye conceal?"

This is a very important point to remember, because Satan is a deceiver. As such he does not want the world to see him as he really is. He is constantly presenting himself as a being more powerful than he really is. He has even presented himself as an angel of light, and his followers as ministers of righteousness.

> [2] *Corinthians 11:14-15* "[14]And no marvel; for Satan himself is transformed into an angel of light.[15] Therefore it is no great thing if his ministers also be transformed as the ministers of righteousness; whose end shall be according to their works."

Please remember that all references to Satan's origin have been omitted from the Quran. Even within Christianity Satan has concealed his true identity. The predominant teaching by the Christian faith is that Satan was the most beautiful Archangel in heaven. When he turned bad he was kicked out of heaven to plague mankind on earth. This teaching comes from Isaiah 14 and Ezekiel 28. Knowing that Satan is not an angel who is it in Isaiah 14 that Satan has tried to equate himself with.

Isaiah 14:11-16 "[11]Thy pomp is brought down *to the grave,* and the noise of thy viols: the worm is spread under thee, and the worms cover thee.[12] How art thou fallen from heaven, O Lucifer, son of the morning! how art thou cut down to the ground, which didst weaken the nations! [13] For thou hast said in thine heart, I will ascend into heaven, I will exalt my throne above the stars of God: I will sit also upon the mount of the congregation, in the sides of the north:[14] I will ascend above the heights of the clouds; I will be like the most High. [15]Yet thou shalt be brought down to hell, to the sides of the pit.[16] They that see thee shall narrowly look upon thee, and consider thee, saying, *Is this the man* that made the earth to tremble, that did shake kingdoms;"

A closer look at Isaiah 14:11 "Thy pomp is brought down to the grave, and the noise of thy viols: the worm is spread under thee, and the worms cover thee."

Definition: *Pomp:* Strong's Number 1347: *Ga'own* (gaw-ohn'); from 1342; the same as 1346: - arrogance, excellence (-lent), majesty, pomp, pride, proud, swelling

The pomp here is the arrogance or majesty of a prince. The individual to whom this verse is referring will go to the *grave*. This cannot be Satan because Revelation 20:7-10 clearly says that Satan will be loosed from the bottomless pit just long enough to be cast into the lake of fire. He never dies and never goes to the grave. Who then is the individual in Isaiah 14? Verse 12 says that this individual had fallen from heaven. The name Lucifer has traditionally been given to Satan means day star, son of the morning. This is supposed to be Satan's angelic name before his demise. However, verse 16 clearly identifies this Lucifer *as a man*. I contend that this can only be—"Adam." For Adam is the only man who fits all these requirements. Satan has never been a man and will never go to the grave.

Now having identified this individual as Adam, who is the individual God is referring to in Ezekiel 28. For the answer to this let's look at verse 2 ; "Son of man, say unto the *prince of Tyrus,* Thus saith the Lord God; Because thine heart is lifted up, and thou hast said, I am a God, I sit in the seat of God, in the midst of the seas; *yet thou art a man, and not God, though thou set thine heart as the heart of God:"* This verse clearly identifies the individual as the same one discussed in Isaiah 14, "Adam;" thou art *a man* and not God." In addition verse 2 calls him the "Prince of Tyrus" who in verse 8 dies and goes to the grave (pit). Now in verse 12, he is referred to as the "King of Tyrus."

> *NOTE:* A prince in heaven has a counterpart on earth called a king. The prince in heaven has more power than the counterpart king on earth. This is another point where my understanding has changed.

Ezekiel 28:11-19 [11] "Moreover the word of the Lord came unto me, saying, [12] Son of man, take up a lamentation upon the King of Tyrus, and say unto him, Thus saith the Lord God; Thou sealest up the sum, full of wisdom, and perfect in beauty. [13] *Thou hast been in Eden the garden of God*; every precious stone was thy covering, the sardius, topaz, and the diamond, the beryl, the onyx, and the jasper, the sapphire, the emerald, and the carbuncle, and gold: the workmanship of thy tabrets and of thy pipes was prepared in thee in the day that thou *wast created.* [14] Thou art the anointed cherub that covereth; and I have set thee so: thou wast upon the holy mountain of God; thou hast walked up and down in the midst of the stones of fire. [15] Thou wast perfect in thy ways from the day that thou wast created, till iniquity was found in thee.[16] By the multitude of thy merchandise they have filled the midst of thee with violence, and thou hast sinned: therefore I will cast thee as profane out of the mountain of God: and I will destroy thee, O covering cherub, from the midst of the stones of fire. [17] *Thine heart was lifted up because of thy beauty, thou hast corrupted thy wisdom by reason of thy brightness: I will cast thee to the ground, I will lay thee before kings, that they may behold thee.*[18] Thou hast defiled thy sanctuaries by the multitude of thine iniquities, by the iniquity of thy traffick; therefore will I bring forth a fire from the midst of thee, it shall devour thee, and *I will bring thee to ashes upon the earth in the sight of all them that behold thee.*[19] All they that know thee among the people shall be astonished at thee: thou shalt be a terror, and never shalt thou be any more."

Ezekiel 28 identifies the Prince of Tyrus and the King of Tyrus as Adam and not Satan. In verse 2 the Prince of Tyrus is called just a man. In verse 13 the King of Tyrus had been, past tense, in the Garden of God and that he was created, therefore not an angel. In verse 17 he became proud and was cast out to the ground. In verse 18 he will return to ashes and therefore is human. Satan will be cast into the lake of fire and does not die. Adam was told by God in Genesis 3:19 that he would return to dust. The word "dust" can also be translated "ashes." The only individual that meets all the requirements of Isaiah 14 and Ezekiel 28 is Adam. In the Garden of Eden Adam was the Prince of Tyrus and on earth he became the King of Tyrus. In his fallen state here on earth Adam took up his counterpart role to his heavenly role of Prince of Tyrus, that of King of Tyrus.

What Is a Counterpart?

What is a counterpart? For now, let's look at Daniel 10, for a short explanation of the meaning. The American Heritage Dictionary defines a counterpart as a person or thing exactly or very much like another, as in function.

> *Daniel 10:1-2* " ¹ "IN the third year of *Cyrus king of Persia* a thing was revealed unto Daniel, whose name was called Belteshazzar; and the thing was true, but the time appointed was long: and he understood the thing, and had understanding of the vision.² In those days I Daniel was mourning *three full weeks.*"

Daniel 10:12-13 "[12] Then said he unto me, Fear not, Daniel: for *from the first day* that thou didst set thine heart to understand, and to chasten thyself before thy God, thy words were heard, and I am come for thy words.[13] But the *prince of the kingdom of Persia* withstood me one and twenty days: but, lo, *Michael, one of the chief princes,* came to help me; and I remained there with the *kings of Persia.*"

Daniel 10:20-21 "[20] Then said he, Knowest thou wherefore I come unto thee? and now will I return to fight with the *prince of Persia:* and when I am gone forth, lo, the *prince of Grecia* shall come.[21] But I will shew thee that which is noted in the scripture of truth: and there is none that holdeth with me in these things, but *Michael your prince.*"

In Daniel 10:1, Cyrus is the *King of Persia (on earth).* Daniel was fasting for three full weeks or 21 days. In verse 12 The angel told him that he was sent on the first day to answer his questions. Also that he did not get there because the *Prince of Persia* prevented him for 20 days. He was able to come to Daniel when Michael (one of the chief princes) intervened and removed the *prince of the kingdom Persia* from blocking the angel. In verse 21 the angel went back to fight with the *Prince of Persia (in heaven)* and when he was gone the *Prince of Grecia* would come. These were events in heaven that happen simultaneously with counterpart events on earth.

Here on earth, Cyrus, the king of Persia has no power to interfere with the movements of an archangel. However, his counterpart in heaven, the prince of Persia, did. The archangel speaking here was assisted by another archangel, Michael. Michael intervened with the prince of Persia and the first archangel continued on his way to Daniel. Notice that there was a conflict in the heavens because the archangel had to return to the fight. It is important to know that there is a war going on in heaven and that this earth and mankind is a vital part of that war. Satan's deception is aimed at interfering with our earthly participation in that war. In verse 21 Michael is identified as the prince of the Jews. Christians have a prince in heaven representing us, his name is Jesus.

Jesus gives us a key to our importance in this war in Matthew 16. It illustrates how we earthly Christians can and do have an effect on the events in heaven.

Matthew 16:16-19 "[19] And Simon Peter answered and said, Thou art the Christ, the Son of the living God.[17] And Jesus answered and said unto him, Blessed art thou, Simon Barjona: for flesh and blood hath not revealed it unto thee, but my Father which is in heaven.[18] And I say also unto thee, That thou art Peter, and upon this rock I will build my church; and the gates of hell shall not prevail against it.[19] And I will give unto thee the *keys of the kingdom of heaven: and whatsoever thou shalt bind on earth shall be bound in heaven; and whatsoever thou shalt loose on earth shall be loosed in heaven.*"

The King of Persia, Cyrus, had a counterpart in the heavens known as the Prince of the kingdom of Persia. The Persian kingdom was conquered by Alexander the Great, a Greek. This Greek king had a counterpart in heaven known as the Prince of the kingdom of Grecia. Here again, an archangel in heaven carries the title of Prince. A prince removed from heaven becomes a king on earth. Thus Jesus is the Prince of Peace and King of Kings. These scriptures, by themselves, demonstrate Mohammed's shallowness of understanding when it came to Holy Bible and Gods purposes.

Adam, prior to his sin and fall was the prince of the Garden of Eden, given the oversight of it in Genesis 2:15, and here in Ezekiel identifies as Tyrus.

Genesis 2:15 "And the Lord God took the man, and put him into the garden of Eden to dress it and to keep it."

Definition: *Dress:* Strong's Number 5647: <u>*Abad*</u> (aw-bad'); a prim. root; to work (in any sense); by impl. to serve, till, (caus.) enslave, etc.: - * be, keep in bondage, be bondmen, bond-service, compel, do, dress, ear, execute, / husbandman, keep, labour (-ing man), bring to pass, (cause to, make to) serve (-ing, self), (be, become) servant (-s), do (use) service, till (-er), transgress [from margin], (set a) work, be wrought, worshipper

Definition: *Keep:* Strong's Number 8401: *Shamar* (shaw-mar'); a prim. root; prop. to hedge about (as with thorns), i. e. guard; gen. to protect, attend to, etc.: - beware, be circumspect, take heed (to self), keep (-er, self), mark, look narrowly, observe, preserve, regard, reserve, save (self), sure, (that lay) wait (for), watch (-man)

After Adam's expulsion from heaven he became a king on the earth and condemned to die. Muhammad denounces this and claims that Adam was forgiven. Therefore, he did not accept the doctrine of the original sin, another one of the satanic deceptions. The purpose of Satan's deception here is clear. With no original sin, there was no need for Jesus to come and cleanse us from the sin that came to us through Adam. With no original sin there is no need of a law requiring a sacrifice (Christ) to remove that sin. The law that Moses brought from God, The Ten Commandments, is totally omitted from the Quran. Muhammad has been deceived by Satan and falls into the condemnation of rejecting Jesus found in *John 3:17-18*

> "17 For God sent not his Son into the world to condemn the world; but that the world through him might be saved. 18 He that believeth on him is not condemned: but he that believeth not is condemned already, because he hath not believed in the name of the only begotten Son of God."

The Old and New Testaments confirm that Jesus was sent to destroy the works of the Devil. Up to the time of Jesus' resurrection, Satan's primary effort was aimed at the Jews. One point is clear, Satan has no power to curse anyone or to make them curse or break God's laws. Therefore, he must deceive them and thereby cause them to bring a curse upon themselves.

The curse is when we sin; we create a separation between us and God. Here is the central reason for Satan's deception of Muhammad. It was Satan that met with Muhammad in the cave, not Gabriel. The proof lies within the Quran as we have seen and we will continue to examine.

It was Satan who gave Muhammad all the teachings found in the Quran, while pretending to be Gabriel. Remember, worst kind of lie is one with an element of truth in it. Satan first revealed his propensity to corrupt the word of God in the Garden of Eden with Eve. He first started with the word of God. Then he creates a doubt that feeds on our weakness. Then he substitutes his polluted version of Gods words and meanings. He did the same thing with Jesus during the forty days in the wilderness. First, he started with the true word of God and then created doubt. "If thou be the son of God, command that these stones be made bread." Jesus answered with these words "it is written." Matthew 4:3-4. In each case Jesus reminded Satan of the "written word of God?" Which is the same word that Muhammad claims was corrupted by the Jews.

For Satan it became clear that he must develop a new set of writings, with Satan as the author, and pass it off as the final and true word of God. Here is where Muhammad enters and the Quran was written but not by the unlearned

Muhammad. Others wrote it long after his death. History records that many disputes over the words of Muhammad and that it was reconstructed "as well as memory would serve." All of this under the orchestration of Satan to obscure the historical account of the Hebrew Bible. The Apostle Paul in *1 Corinthians 10:11* refers to the Hebrews while they were still in the wilderness as an example for today concerning the end of the world. This includes the end of Satan and his followers.

> [1] *Corinthians 10:11*
> "Now all these things happened unto them for ensamples; and they are written for our admonition, upon whom the ends of the world are come."

Everything that happened to the Hebrews was for types, examples and patterns for us to understand what the end of the world is to be like.

With this in mind Satan could look forward to the written word in *Revelations 20:10*

> "And the devil that deceived them was cast into the lake of fire and brimstone, where the beast

and the false prophet are, and shall be torment-
ed day and night for ever and ever."

Knowing his end is written Satan has sought to change the written word of God to save his life. Of course this is wishful thinking on his part. Common sense and logical thinking have not been one of Satan's strong points. If it were he would never have encouraged the Jews to crucify Jesus and thereby seal his fate.

When a close inspection of the Quran is made, we find that every major doctrine, that Christian's and Jews hold sacred, is corrupted. There are only two times in which God personally wrote in the scriptures. It was the finger of God that wrote the Ten Commandments on tablets of stone. The exclusion of these commandments can only mean that Muhammad supersedes even the written word of God. The Quran even alters the events that establish those doctrines. Jesus, during His temptations in the wilderness, quoted the written word of God to rebuke Satan.

It is my belief that Satan has convinced himself into believing that if he can change the written word of God, he can save his life. The outcome of this deception plays heavily upon our present day, all of which is another topic of another book.

Chapter 11

Conclusion

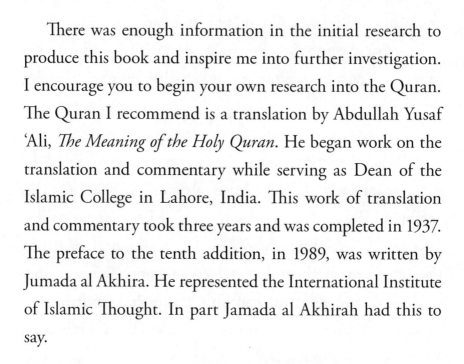

There was enough information in the initial research to produce this book and inspire me into further investigation. I encourage you to begin your own research into the Quran. The Quran I recommend is a translation by Abdullah Yusaf 'Ali, *The Meaning of the Holy Quran*. He began work on the translation and commentary while serving as Dean of the Islamic College in Lahore, India. This work of translation and commentary took three years and was completed in 1937. The preface to the tenth addition, in 1989, was written by Jumada al Akhira. He represented the International Institute of Islamic Thought. In part Jamada al Akhirah had this to say.

"The tremendous impact that this work has made upon the English-reading Muslims (as well as, many non-Muslims) of the world, has never been greater than it is today and shall continue—in sha'a Allah (Allah willing) for generations to come."

Abdullah's translation has footnotes explaining how the text is to be applied and why. It also has appendages that review the historical background, as Islam views it. In addition, it reveals how Islam applies current archeological discoveries as they relate to the historical accounts recorded within the Quran.

The Quran is very tenacious about its overriding authority with regard to the Hebrew Bible (Old Testament) and the New Testament. However, that authority does not negate them altogether. They are important to the doctrine of Islam as they are applied, in part, to bolster the claims of the Quran and Muhammad. At Muhammad's instruction the Quran was to be added to the Old and New Testaments to form what he [Muhammad] calls the whole book of Allah. Muhammad claims that both the Old and New Testaments are corrupted. However, as corrupted as he claims, he uses parts of them to support his declaration as the seal of the prophets and the Quran as the final word of God. To research the validity of these claims a standard set of discipline, or criticism are applied. The criticisms applied here are identical to the disciplines use to establish the validity of the Holy Bible. A modern approach to the Biblical studies incorporates a literary criticism, a form criticism, a redaction criticism and a historical criticism. Each of these methods does not exclude the others. They are in part mutually complementary.

When you apply the same disciplines of criticisms, *discussions about the qualities of a creative work,* used to study the Holy Bible to the Quran, does the Quran meet the same standard? When applying the Literary Criticism of authorship to the Quran you find the question of authorship is not resolved. When the authorship of a book within the Holy Bible is not clear or unknown it is so stated. The authorship of the Quran is credited solely to Muhammad. However, he died one year before the work of compiling and editing the elements of the Quran began. The fact of his illiteracy cannot be overlooked. Even if he had been alive when the Quran was competed, he could not have proof read it for accuracy of thought and content. Even though the verses are credited to him there is some doubt. Ali Bekr, Muhammad's successor did not begin the compiling of Muhammad's teaching until one year after his death. At that time his instructions were to *write down Muhammad's teachings as well as memory could serve.* It appears that the same people who were reconstructing Muhammad's teaching were compiling a book called the Sunna. We know that the Sunna is plagued with miss quotes and distortions that served the political interests of those who wrote it.

The area to Form Criticism questions continuity within the literary genre. The Quran emphatically asserts that the genre used by it was to prevent any misunderstandings or corruption. Surah 19:97 declares the clarity of understanding through the language used.

"So have we made
The (Quran) easy
In thine own tongue.
That with it thou mayest give
Glad tidings to the righteous,
And warning to the people
Given to contention."

Surah 15:9 asserts Allah's personal protection of the Quran from corruption.

"We have, without doubt,
Sent down the Message:
And We will assuredly
Guard it (from corruption)."

The creditability of these verses falls into question as no Arab, in Muhammad's day, would be using the words *thine, thou, and mayest.* These words came from the old English vernacular used in the time of King James. They are used in the King James translation of Holy Bible in 1611 A.D. These words were assuredly not in Muhammad's own tongue.

The Redaction Criticism studies the Quran in its final form. There is no doubt of Muhammad's contribution to the Quran. Confusion sets in when we consider how the material was collected, compiled, edited and put in its final form. Again, Ali Bekr's waited one year after Muhammad's death to begin the process. His instruction to write down the prophets sayings as "well as memory could serve" presents many unanswered questions. Who and how many people were involved in the process? Who was entrusted with the collection of the material? Who compiled the material into the chapter and verse arrangement within the Quran? Muhammad recited the text over a 13 year period. Did he recite an entire Surah before going on to the next or were the verses given in a sporadic manner? If so who arranged them in the order we have today?

The final version produced did not appear until Ultman, Muhammad's third successor, released it. The question of who edited this final version, of Muhammad's time, remains unanswered. Accordingly, the translation produced by Abdullah Yusaf 'Ali does not resolve this situation.

The Quran that was released by Ultman was written without vowels to define the meanings of some words. Because of this seven or more different Qurans were in use. It was not until 1924, 1200+ years later that an Egyptian rendering was produced that was acceptable to the Islamic world. The purity of the text produced by Abdullah Yusaf 'Ali is questioned because of his use of words like thee, thine and mayest.

Entered here is just a few of the questions revealed by a preliminary examination and should lay the groundwork for an in-depth research. This first round examination through the basics of the disciplines, Literary Criticism, Form Criticism, Redaction Criticism and Historical Criticism, uncovers a work of confusion and contradiction.

Since the Quran is to be added to the Hebrew Bible and the New Testament to form the "Whole Book of Allah." It would be logical to believe the accounts in all three would be compatible, as God is supposed to be the source of inspiration for all of them. All three books acknowledge God as the only supreme power. With God being the supreme power and originator of all three books, how is it that the Hebrew Bible and the New Testament accounts are in unison. While the Qurans accounts are not in harmony with either the Old and New Testaments of God.

This initial comparison between the Holy Bible and the Quran has revealed that major doctrines of the Holy Bible have been omitted from the Quran. For example, the biblical account of the Ten Commandments (Exodus 24:12) has been omitted.

The importance of the Ten Commandments cannot be disregarded. How could Muhammad's Gabriel forget the direct input to the Holy Bible from God? Here in Exodus 24 we find that God personally wrote the Ten Commandments on tablets of stone.

> *Exodus 24:12*
>
> "12 And the LORD said unto Moses, Come up to me into the mount, and be there: and I will give thee tables of stone, and a law, and commandments which I have written; that thou mayest teach them."

If the Jews corrupted the scriptures as Muhammad claimed. How is it that Muhammad's Gabriel did not include the Ten Commandments in the revelations from God? It is the Ten Commandments that forbid the idolatry of the Kaaba rituals and the black stone of Mecca. It is the Ten Commandments that forbids adultery, murder, stealing, bearing false witness and coveting someone else's property. Jesus certifies the Ten Commandments in New Testament times. How is it that the Quran omits them and condones the actions they forbid?

The Saudi funded schools in Alexandria VA. Teaches grades K-12 that these things are acceptable to God. Through the schools direct involvement in the Public School textbook publications, they have produced a sanitized version of a peaceful Islam, glossing over its violent nature. Easy access to heaven through acts of violence towards God's enemies is guaranteed. Rewards in heaven and access to it are distorted within the Quran.

The Hebrew Bible and the New Testament states that the things God has prepared for those who love Him, have not entered into to the hearts or minds of man.

Isaiah 64:4
"⁴ For since the beginning of the world *men* have not heard, nor perceived by the ear, neither hath the eye seen, O God, beside thee, *what* he hath prepared for him that waiteth for him."

¹ *Corinthians 2:9*
"⁹ But as it is written, Eye hath not seen, nor ear heard, neither have entered into the heart of man, the things which God hath prepared for them that love him."

One contradiction arises as the Quran spends a great deal of time describing mans reward in heaven. Each individual's rewards are centered on the fleshly desires of men, provided by women. Muslims are assured entrance into heavens highest reward, if they die fighting the enemies of Allah. The standard of morality lived by the individual is not considered. The individual can be the greatest of sinners and bypass the judgment day and obtain the highest reward possible.

In Surshs 8 and 60, the Quran teaches, anyone who is not part of Islam (Muslim) is unbelievers. They are to be harassed and terrorized until they convert to Islam. All Muslims are instructed to continue this practice until there is only one, worldwide Islamic state.

Current public awareness has been kindled as the teachings of Muhammad's day have surfaced in our time. The events that happened then are repeating themselves now. How is it, such a thing could happen here and now? How could the facts of Muhammad's day have been altered or modified today? For instance, Muhammad is known to have started the religion of the sword. Due to the efforts of Susan L. Douglas, a teacher at the Saudi Funded Alexandria Academy in Alexandria VA., this fact has been deleted from our public school textbooks. The result is a presentation of an Islam that is more peaceful than it is. This is a presentation that displays an Islam that is heavily concerned about human rights and the rights of women.

The lack of human rights in Islamic theocracies is horrifying. Women are relegated to third class and no class status. The harshness and intolerance of Sharia law can be observed in the stoning of women and the cruelty of punishment for minor infractions. Peoples of other faiths are tortured and killed. Young Christian girls are kidnapped and forced into Islamic marriages against their will. The Voice of the Martyrs, P.O. Box 443, Bartlesville Oklahoma 74005-0443 publishes a monthly report on these situations.

The Quran condones and encourages this in Surahs 8:59-60 and 8:38-39.

Surah 8:59-60 Pages 428-429

"⁵⁹ Let not the Unbelievers
Think that they can
Get the better (of the godly),
They will never frustrate (them).
⁶⁰ Against them make ready
Your strength to the utmost
Of your power, to strike terror
Into (the hearts of) the enemies

Of Allah and your enemies

And others besides, whom

Allah doth know. Whatever

Ye shall spend in the Cause

Of Allah, shall be repaid

Unto you, and ye shall not

Be treated unjustly."[1227]

Footnote 1226 Page 429

"There are always lurking enemies whom you may not know, but whom Allah knows. *It is your duty to be ready against all, for the sacred Cause under whose banner you are fighting.*"

Surah 8:38-39 Page 423

[38] "Say to the Unbelievers,

If (now) they desist (from Unbelief),

Their past would be forgiven them;

But if they persist, the punishment

Of those before them is already

(A matter of warning for them).

[39] "And fight them on

Until there is no more

Tumult or oppression,

And there prevails

Justice and faith in Allah[1207]
Altogether and everywhere;
But if they cease, verily Allah
Doth se all that they do."[1208]

Footnote 1208 Page 423

"If they cease from fighting and from persecution of truth. Allah judges them by their actions and their motives, and would not wish that they should be *harassed with further hostility.* But if they refuse all terms, the righteous have nothing to fear: Allah will help protect them."

Here Muslims are taught to strike terror in the hearts of their enemies. This practice was used in Muhammad's day and it continues today. This doctrine of the Quran, fueled by the holy jihad has this present day world snared in war.

The holy jihad is a doctrine that came to life with Muhammad and it lives today. As you research the history and use of the jihad, more confusion sets in. We know how Muhammad is connected to the jihad and how he used it in his day. How is that doctrine of the Quran applied today here in the United States? For part of the answer we can look at

Susan L. Douglas. In her position as historical instructor at the Saudi funded Islamic academy in Alexandria, Virginia. She has made a direct impact upon our public school curriculum concerning the holy jihad. She is also a consultant for the CIE, Council on Islamic Education, and responsible for part of the change in our public school history textbooks. She is active in promoting a glossed over version of the holy jihad and presenting more peaceful image of Islam within our school textbooks. WorldnetDaily.com posted an article on Susan Douglas and John L. Esposito; the following are quotes from that article:

> "In her position as "principal researcher and writer" for the Council on Islamic Education (CIE). She has been instrumental in convincing "American textbook publishers and educators to gloss over the violent aspect of Islam to make the faith more appealing to non-Muslim children. The units on Islam reviewed by WorldNetDaily appear to give a glowing and largely uncritical view of the faith."

> "Even scholar John L Esposito, considered by critics to be one of Islam's leading apologists has written that "jihad means the struggle to

spread and defend Islam"—through "warfare" if necessary."

Now we see how the religion of the Quran is using deception to advance itself into a worldwide Islamic state.

The Quran teaches that the final punishment for unbelievers is the lake of fire. Revelation 21:8 agrees with that assessment. It also states that those included in the list designated for the lake of fire is "all liars."

> *Revelation 21:8*
> [8] But the fearful, and unbelieving, and the abominable, and murderers, and whoremongers, and sorcerers, and idolaters, and *all liars*, shall have their part in the lake which burneth with fire and brimstone: which is the second death.

The Greek word used here for liars is pseudes (psyoo-dace') meaning untrue, deceitful and false. It is evident that Muslims feel no guilt in perpetuating a false image of Islam. This is an image that conceals its hostile and aggressive nature behind a veil of peace and goodwill. God has pronounced the end result of those who live by falsehood, the lake of fire.

The question arises as to who would be so brazened as to advance a teaching that is diametrically opposed to God's will. A will that is set down in God's own hand writing, written on the stone tablets of the Ten Commandments and given to Moses. The Ten Commandments are opposed to that individual's purpose. Could this be the reason the Ten Commandments have been omitted from the Quran? Could this be one of the reasons for Islam's rapid growth?

Islam is the fastest growing religion in the world. Based on the teachings of Muhammad written in the Quran, Islam is advancing. The Quran is a curious mixture of the Old Testament, New Testament, Greek culture of Alexander the Great and the pre-Islamic Paganism of Mecca from which Muhammad came.

This comparison of the Holy Bible and the Quran is not complete. The presentation here reveals a Quran that is fundamentally opposed to all that God has declared holy. The Quran instructs a people to preach peace and practice war. They terrorize all people who dare to disagree with its teachings. Political correctness is a mighty tool used in this war.

Even in the basic stages of a critical study the Quran could not stand up to the same scrutiny as the Holy Bible.

The deception of Satan is seen in the actions of the Islamic people. When in a minority they are peaceful and use political correctness to practice and advance the religion. When they gain the majority and believe they have the upper hand, they will terrorize and harass until the enemy relents and converts to Islam. Don't just take my word for it; look around you at current world events.

Look at the countries where Islam is ascendant, where the Islamic theocracy rules. Do you see prosperity, equality and fairness? Are women treated like merchandise to be traded, and the horrors of Sharia law the way of life? Do you see cruelty and violence against anyone who "strays from the straight path.?" Do you find people living in a cruel world of confusion? Is this the true image of the doctrines of the Quran?

How can anyone call this the will of God? That mankind, who God formed out of the dust of the ground, should be so abased by mankind.

It was stated earlier that what Muslims share with non-Muslims about the Quran, Islam and Muhammad is confusing to say the least. Confusion does not come from God; He is not the author of confusion. Confusion comes from Satan and he uses it to destroy.

1 Corinthians 14:33

[33] For God is not *the author* of confusion, but of peace, as in all churches of the saints.

James 3:13-18

[13] Who *is* a wise man and endued with knowledge among you? let him shew out of a good conversation his works with meekness of wisdom. [14] But if ye have bitter envying and strife in your hearts, glory not, and lie not against the truth. [15] This wisdom descendeth not from above, but *is* earthly, sensual, devilish. [16] *For where envying and strife is, there is confusion and every evil work.* [17] But the wisdom that is from above is first pure, then peaceable, gentle, *and* easy to be intreated, full of mercy and good fruits, without partiality, and without hypocrisy. [18] And the fruit of righteousness is sown in peace of them that make peace.

One thing is for certain, the farther your research goes the number of questions will keep mounting. Nothing is ever completely resolved and confusion mounts. Start your inquiry; you can begin with the following list of question. See if you can find the answers?

- Who would be behind the list of deceptions found in the Quran?

- Who would gain the most by such a deception?

- What would be the motive behind the deception?

- What would this individual gain by destroying the faith of the Holy Bible?

- What would the one behind the deception gain by forcing everyone into renouncing their faith in favor of Islam?

- Why is it that anyone who renounces Islam for another faith is condemned to die?

- Why it is that Islam gets violent when anyone questions the Quran and Muhammad?

- Why it is that Islam demands tolerance of its practices and beliefs yet is intolerant of all others?

May God the Father of our Lord Jesus the Christ bless you and guide you on your search for truth. I leave you with this thought.

The Quran, is it Gods word or a satanic deception, you be the judge.

John W. Tharp

Bibliography

1. 'Abdullah Yusuf 'Ali. *The Meaning of the Holy Quran*: amana/publicantions, 10th Edition, 1999.

2. Braswell, Jr, George W. *Islam, Its Prophet, Peoples, Politics, and Power*. Broadman and Holman Publishers, Nashville, Tennessee, 1996

3. Bromiley, Goeffrey W., *The International Standard Bible Encyclopedia*: Volume A-D, by William B. Eerdmans Publishing Com., Grand Rapids, MI 1979.

4. Bruce, F. F. *The Canon of Scripture*: InterVarsity Pres, Downers Grove, Illinois, 1988.

5. Bruce M. Metzger and Roland E. Murphy. *The New Oxford Annotated Bible*, New Revised Standard Version, Oxford University Press, 1991

6. Elwell, Walter A. *Baker Encyclopedia of the Bible*: Volume I, E.G., Baker Books, Grand Rapids, MI., 1998.

7. "Encarta." Encyclopedia; Microsoft, 1993-2003

8. "Encarta." Encyclopedia; Microsoft, 2005

9. Garrett, Jr., James Leo, and William B. Eerdmans. *Systematic Theology.* Volume I, by Publishing Co., Grand Rapids, MI, 1990.

10. Grudem, Wayne. *Systematic Theology.* Zondervan Publishing House, Grand Rapids, MI, 1994.

11. Hodge, Charles. *Systematic Theology.* Volume I, William B. Eerdmans Publishing Com., Grand Rapids, MI 1982.

12. Martin, William C.. *The Layman's Bible Encyclopedia.* The Southwestern Company, Nashville, TN., 1964.

13. Martinez, Florentino Garcia, *The Dead Sea Scrolls Translated, The Qumran Texts in English.* Second Edition. E. J. Brill Leiden, New York Cologne, William B. Eerdmans, Grand Rapids, MI. 1996

14. Murphy, E. F. Thomas. *Handbook for Spiritual Warfare.* Nealson Publishers, 1977, c1996

15. Myres, Philip VanNess. *Ancient History:* 2nd Edition; Ginn and Company; New York, NY; 1904 and 1916

16. Parker, James I. and Merrill C. Tenney, and William White Jr.. *The Bible Almanac.* Thomas Nelson Publishers, Nashville, TN., 1980

17. Pickthall, Marmaduke William Muhammad. *Meaning of the Glorious Quran.* London, 1937.

18. Richardson, Allen and John Bowden. *The Wesminister Dictionary of Christian Theology.* The Westminister Press, Philadelphia, PA, 1983

19. Strong's, James, LL,D., S.T.D. 1822-1894. *The New Strong's Exhaustive Concordance.* Thomas Nelson Publishers, Nashville, Tennessee, 1984

20. Suskino, Richard: AW.W. Norton Book; *The Sward of the Prophet.* Gosset and Dunlap, New York, New York 1972

21. Thompson, by Frank Charles DD, Ph D; B.B. *The Thompson Chain-Reference Bible:* KJV, 4th Edition; Kirkbride Bible Co., Inc., Indianapolis IN; 1957

22. Wallbank, T. Walter and Alastair M. Taylor. *Civilization Past and Present*. The University of Southern California; Scott, Foresman and Company; Volume I; 1942

23. Young, E. S. BA, B.D. *The Bible Geography*. Brethren Publishing House, Elgin ILL, 1899

24. Zaxhary, John. *Gabriel's Faces*. Prophesy in the News,